Presented To:

Mom

With love,

From:

Susan

Date:

December 25, 1998

A Treasury of Christmas Classics

Honor Books
Tulsa, Oklahoma

Unless otherwise indicated, all Scripture quotations are taken from the *King James Version* of the Bible.

Editor's Note: Some stories have been adapted, translated, or changed slightly for clarity or for spacing. However, in all instances, every effort was made to maintain the original message and intent of the story.

A Treasury of Christmas Classics
ISBN 1-56292-360-9
Copyright © 1997 by Honor Books, Inc.
P. O. Box 55388
Tulsa, OK 74155

Manuscript prepared by W. B. Freeman Concepts, Inc., Tulsa, Oklahoma.

Introduction

What a Season!

Christmas! The very sound of the word brings joy to most people's hearts.

Christmas has become synonymous with giving, feasts and festivities, bright lights and abundant sweets, carolers and candles, family and friends.

May this collection inspire within you a sense of the eternal and a desire to make each day of the holiday season a special one of praise and thanksgiving. This unforgettable collection is overflowing with all-time favorite stories, poems, essays, and prayers that will fill your heart with Christmas cheer.

May this Christmas treasury remind you continually of God's great love for you and all people. May it kindle anew within your own heart a deeper desire to love God, as well as to express genuine love to others.

Read these stories aloud to your children. Read them aloud to yourself. Enjoy! After all, 'tis the season for joy.

TABLE OF CONTENTS

A Treasury
of Classic
Prayers
for Christmas

Prayers for Christmas

*I*n a world that seems not only to be changing, but even to be dissolving, there are some tens of millions of us who want Christmas to be the same . . . with the same old greeting "Merry Christmas" and no other.

We long for the abiding love among men of goodwill which the season brings . . . believing in this ancient miracle of Christmas with its softening, sweetening influence to tug at our heartstrings once again.

We want to hold on to the old customs and traditions because they strengthen our family ties, bind us to our friends, make us one with all mankind for whom the Child was born, and bring us back again to the God Who gave His only begotten Son, that "whosoever believeth in Him should not perish, but have everlasting life."

So we will not "spend" Christmas . . . nor "observe" Christmas.

We will "keep" Christmas — keep it as it is . . . in all the loveliness of its ancient traditions.

May we keep it in our hearts, that we may be kept in its hope.

— Peter Marshall

Prayers for Christmas

Compassionate and holy God,
we celebrate with joy your coming into our midst;
we celebrate with hope your coming into our midst;
we celebrate with peace your coming into our midst;
for you have come to save us.
By your grace we recognize your presence in men and women
in all parts of your world . . .
through your strength our lives can proclaim joy and hope;
through your love we can work for peace and justice.

You are the source of our being;
you are the light of our lives.

— Based on lines from a Latin American Prayer

Loving Father, help us remember the birth of Jesus, that we may
share in the song of the angels, the gladness of the shepherds and
the wisdom of the wise men.

Close the door of hate and open the door of love all over the world.

Let kindness come with every gift and good desires with every greeting.

Deliver us from evil by the blessing which Christ brings and teach us
to be merry with clean hearts.

May the Christmas morning make us happy to be your children and
the Christmas evening bring us to our beds with grateful thoughts,
forgiving and forgiven, for Jesus' sake.

Amen.

— Robert Louis Stevenson

Prayers for Christmas

Christmas peace is God's; and he must give it himself, with his own hand, or we shall never get it. Go then to God himself. Thou art his child, as Christmas Day declares; be not afraid to go unto thy Father. Pray to him; tell him what thou wantest: say, "Father, I am not moderate, reasonable, forbearing. I fear I cannot keep Christmas aright for I have not a peaceful Christmas spirit in me; and I know that I shall never get it by thinking, and reading, and understanding; for it passes all that, and lies far away beyond it, does peace, in the very essence of thine undivided, unmoved, absolute, eternal Godhead, which no change nor decay of this created world, nor sin or folly of men or devils, can ever alter; but which abideth forever what it is, in perfect rest, and perfect power and perfect love. O Father, give me thy Christmas peace.

— Charles Kingsley

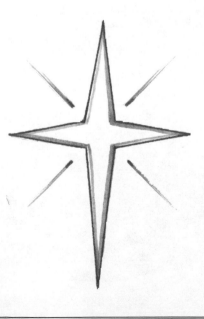

Prayers for Christmas

O God, You make us glad by the yearly festival of the birth of your only Son Jesus Christ: Grant that we, who joyfully receive him as our Redeemer, may with sure confidence behold him when he comes to be our Judge; who lives and reigns with you and the Holy Spirit, one God, now and forever. *Amen*.

O God, you have caused this holy night to shine with the brightness of the true Light: Grant that we, who have known the mystery of that Light on earth, may also enjoy him perfectly in heaven; where with you and the Holy Spirit he lives and reigns, one God, in glory everlasting. *Amen*.

Almighty God, you have given your only begotten Son to take our nature upon him, and to be born of a pure virgin: Grant that we, who have been born again and made your children by adoption and grace, may daily be renewed by your Holy Spirit, through our Lord Jesus Christ, to whom with you and the same Spirit be honor and glory, now and forever. *Amen*.

— *The Book of Common Prayer*

A Treasury of Classic Stories for Christmas

HEYWOOD BROUN

A Shepherd

The host of heaven and the angel of the Lord had filled the sky with radiance. Now the glory of God was gone and the shepherds and the sheep stood under dim starlight. The men were shaken by the wonders they had seen and heard and, like the animals, they huddled close.

"Let us now," said the eldest of the shepherds, "go even unto Bethlehem, and see this thing which has come to pass, which the Lord hath made known unto us."

The City of David lay beyond a far, high hill upon the crest of which there danced a star. The men made haste to be away, but as they broke out of the circle there was one called Amos who remained. He dug his crook into the turf and clung to it.

"Come," cried the eldest of the shepherds, but Amos shook his head. They marveled, and one called out, "It is true. It was an angel. You heard the tidings. A Savior is born!"

"I heard," said Amos. "I will abide."

The eldest walked back from the road to the little knoll on which Amos stood.

"You do not understand," the old man told him. "We have a sign from God. An angel commanded us. We go to worship the Savior, who is even now born in Bethlehem. God has made His will manifest."

"It is not in my heart," replied Amos.

And now the eldest of the shepherds was angry.

"With your own eyes," he cried out, "you have seen the host of heaven in these dark hills. And you heard, for it was like the thunder when 'Glory to God in the highest' came ringing to us out of the night."

And again Amos said, "It is not in my heart."

Another shepherd then broke in. "Because the hills still stand and the sky has not fallen, it is not enough for Amos. He must have something louder than the voice of God."

Amos held more tightly to his crook and answered, "I have need of a whisper."

They laughed at him and said, "What should this voice say in your ear?"

He was silent and they pressed about him and shouted mockingly, "Tell us now. What says the God of Amos, the little shepherd of a hundred sheep?"

Meekness fell away from him. He took his hands from off the crook and raised them high.

"I too am a god," said Amos in a loud, strange voice, "and to my hundred sheep I am a savior."

And when the din of the angry shepherds about him slackened, Amos pointed to his hundred.

"See my flock," he said. "See the fright of them. The fear of the bright angel and of the voices is still upon them. God is busy in Bethlehem. He has no time for a hundred sheep. They are my sheep. I will abide."

This the others did not take so much amiss, for they saw that there was a terror in all the flocks and they too knew the ways of sheep. And before the shepherds departed on the road to Bethlehem toward the bright star, each talked to Amos and told him what he should do for the care of the several flocks. And yet one or two turned back a moment to taunt Amos, before they reached the dip in the road which led to the City of David. It was said, "We shall see new glories at the throne of God, and you, Amos, you will see sheep."

Amos paid no heed, for he thought to himself, "One shepherd the less will not matter at the throne of God." Nor did he have time to be troubled that he was not to see the Child who was come to save the world. There was much to be done among the flocks and Amos walked between the sheep and made under his tongue a clucking noise, which was a way he had, and to his hundred and to the others it was a sound more fine and friendly than the voice of the bright angel. Presently the animals ceased to tremble and they began to graze as the sun came up over the hill where the star had been.

"For sheep," said Amos to himself, "the angels shine too much. A shepherd is better."

With the morning the others came up the road from Bethlehem, and they told Amos of the manger and of the wise men who had mingled there with shepherds. And they described to him the gifts: gold, frankincense and myrrh. And when they were done they said, "And did you see wonders here in the fields with the sheep?"

Amos told them, "Now my hundred are one hundred and one," and he showed them a lamb which had been born just before the dawn.

"Was there for this a great voice out of heaven?" asked the eldest of the shepherds.

Amos shook his head and smiled, and there was upon his face that which seemed to the shepherds a wonder even in a night of wonders.

"To my heart," he said, "there came a whisper."

The Little Loaf

Once, when there was a famine, a rich baker sent for twenty of the poorest children in the town and said to them, "In this basket there is a loaf for each of you. Take it, and come back to me every day till God sends us better times."

The hungry children gathered eagerly about the basket, and quarreled for the bread, because each wished to have the largest loaf. At last they went away without even thanking the good man.

But Gretchen, a poorly dressed little girl, did not quarrel or struggle with the rest, but remained standing modestly a pace away. When the ill-behaved children had left, she took the smallest loaf, which alone was left in the basket, kissed the man's hand, and went home.

The next day the children were as ill-behaved as before, and poor, timid Gretchen received a loaf scarcely half the size of the one she got the first day. When she came home, and her mother cut the loaf open, many new, shining pieces of silver fell out of it.

The mother was very much alarmed, and said, "Take the money back to the good man at once, for it must have got in the dough by accident. Go quickly, Gretchen, go quickly!" But when the little girl gave the rich man her mother's message, he said, "No, no, my child, it was no mistake. I had the silver pieces put into the smallest loaf to reward you. Always be contented, peaceable; and grateful as you are now. Go home, now, and tell your mother that the money is your own.

O. HENRY

The Gift of the Magi

One dollar and eighty-seven cents. That was all. And sixty cents of it was in pennies. Pennies saved one and two at a time by bulldozing the grocer and the vegetable man and the butcher until one's cheeks burned with the silent imputation of parsiomony that such close dealing implied. Three times Della counted it. One dollar and eighty-seven cents. And the next day would be Christmas.

There was clearly nothing to do but flop down on the shabby little couch and howl. So Della did it. Which instigates the moral reflection that life is made up of sobs, sniffles, and smiles, with sniffles predominating.

While the mistress of the home is gradually subsiding from the first stage to the second, take a look at the home. A furnished flat at $8 a week. It did not exactly fit a beggar's description, but it certainly had that word on the lookout for the mendicancy squad.

In the vestibule below was a letter box into which no letter would go, and an electric button from which no mortal finger could coax a ring. Also appertaining thereunto was a card bearing the name "Mr. James Dillingham Young."

The "Dillingham" had been flung to the breeze during a former period of prosperity when its possessor was being paid $30 per week.

Now, when the income was shrunk to $20, the letters of "Dillingham" looked blurred, as though they were thinking seriously of contracting to a modest and unassuming D. But whenever Mr. James Dillingham Young came home and reached his flat above he was called "Jim" and greatly hugged by Mrs. James Dillingham Young, already introduced to you as Della. Which is all very good.

Della finished her cry and attended to her cheeks with the powder rag. She stood by the window and looked out dully at a grey cat walking to a grey fence in a grey backyard. Tomorrow would be Christmas Day, and she had only $1.87 with which to buy Jim a present. She had been saving every penny she could for months, with this result. Twenty dollars a week doesn't go far. Expenses had been greater than she had calculated. They always are. Only $1.87 to buy a present for Jim. Her Jim. Many a happy hour she had spent planning for something nice for him. Something fine and rare and sterling — something just a little bit near to being worthy of the honour of being owned by Jim.

There was a pierglass between the windows of the room. Perhaps you have seen a pierglass in an $8 flat. A very thin and very agile person may, by observing his reflection in a rapid sequence of longitudinal strips, obtain a fairly accurate conception of his looks. Della, being slender, had mastered the art.

Suddenly she whirled from the window and stood before the glass. Her eyes were shining brilliantly, but her face had lost its colour within twenty seconds. Rapidly she pulled down her hair and let it fall to its full length.

Now, there were two possessions of the James Dillingham Youngs in which they both took a mighty pride. One was Jim's gold watch that had been his father's and grandfather's. The other was Della's hair. Had the Queen of Sheba lived in the flat across the airshaft, Della would have let her hair hang out the window some day to dry just to depreciate Her Majesty's jewels and gifts. Had King Solomon been the janitor, with all his treasures piled up in the basement, Jim would have pulled out his watch every time he passed, just to see him pluck at his beard from envy.

So now Della's beautiful hair fell about her, rippling and shining like a cascade of brown waters. It reached below her knee and made itself almost a garment for her. And then she did it up again nervously and quickly. Once she faltered for a minute and stood still while a tear or two splashed on the worn red carpet.

On went her old brown jacket; on went her old brown hat. With a whirl of skirts and with the brilliant sparkle still in her eyes, she fluttered out the door and down the stairs to the street.

Where she stopped the sign read: "Mme. Sofronie. Hair Goods of All Kinds." One flight up Della ran, and collected herself, panting. Madame, large, too white, chilly, hardly looked the "Sofronie."

"Will you buy my hair?" asked Della.

"I buy hair," said Madame. "Take yer hat off and let's have a sight at the looks of it."

Down rippled the brown cascade.

"Twenty dollars," said Madame, lifting the mass with a practiced hand.

"Give it to me quick," said Della.

Oh, and the next two hours tripped by on rosy wings. Forget the hashed metaphor. She was ransacking the stores for Jim's present.

She found it at last. It surely had been made for Jim and no one else. There was no other like it in any of the stores, and she had turned all of them inside out. It was a platinum fob chain simple and chaste in design, properly proclaiming its value by substance alone and not by meretricious ornamentation — as all good things should do. It was even worthy of The Watch. As soon as she saw it she knew that it must be Jim's. It was like him. Quietness and value — the description applied to both. Twenty-one dollars they took from her for it, and she hurried home with the 87 cents. With that chain on his watch Jim might be properly anxious about the time in any company. Grand as the watch was, he sometimes looked at it on the sly on account of the old leather strap that he used in place of a chain.

When Della reached home her intoxication gave way a little to prudence and reason. She got out her curling irons and lighted the gas and went to work repairing the ravages made by generosity added to love. Which is always a tremendous task, dear friends — a mammoth task.

Within forty minutes her head was covered with tiny, close-lying curls that made her look wonderfully like a truant schoolboy. She looked at her reflection in the mirror long, carefully, and critically.

"If Jim doesn't kill me," she said to herself, "before he takes a second look at me, he'll say I look like a Coney Island chorus girl. But what could I do — oh! what could I do with a dollar and eighty-seven cents?"

At 7 o'clock the coffee was made and the frying-pan was on the back of the stove hot and ready to cook the chops.

Jim was never late. Della doubled the fob chain in her hand and sat on the corner of the table near the door that he always entered. Then she heard his step on the stair away down on the first flight, and she turned white for just a moment. She had a habit of saying little silent prayers about the simplest everyday things, and now she whispered: "Please God, make him think I am still pretty."

The door opened and Jim stepped in and closed it. He looked thin and very serious. Poor fellow, he was only twenty-two — and to be burdened with a family! He needed a new overcoat and he was without gloves.

Jim stopped inside the door, as immovable as a setter at the scent of quail. His eyes were fixed upon Della, and there was an expression in them that she could not read, and it terrified her. It was not anger, nor surprise, nor disapproval, nor horror, nor any of the sentiments that she had been prepared for. He simply stared at her fixedly with that peculiar expression on his face.

Della wriggled off the table and went for him.

"Jim, darling," she cried, "don't look at me that way. I had my hair cut off and sold it because I couldn't have lived through Christmas without giving you a present. It'll grow out again — you won't mind, will you? I just had to do it. My hair grows awfully fast. Say 'Merry Christmas!' Jim, and let's be happy. You don't know what a nice — what a beautiful, nice gift I've got for you."

"You've cut off your hair?" asked Jim, laboriously, as if he had not arrived at that patent fact yet even after the hardest mental labour.

"Cut it off and sold it," said Della. "Don't you like me just as well, anyhow? I'm me without my hair, aint' I?"

Jim looked about the room curiously.

"You say your hair is gone?" he said, with an air almost of idiocy.

"You needn't look for it," said Della. "It's sold, I tell you — sold and gone, too. It's Christmas Eve, boy. Be good to me, for it went for you. Maybe the hairs of my head were numbered," she went on with a sudden serious sweetness, "but nobody could ever count my love for you. Shall I put the chops on, Jim?"

Out of his trance Jim seemed quickly to wake. He enfolded his Della. For ten seconds let us regard with discreet scrutiny some inconsequential object in the other direction. Eight dollars a week or a million a year — what is the difference? A mathematician or a wit would give you the wrong answer. The magi brought valuable gifts, but that was not among them. This dark assertion will be illuminated later on.

Jim drew a package from his overcoat pocket and threw it upon the table.

"Don't make any mistake, Dell," he said, "about me. I don't think there's anything in the way of a haircut or a shave or a shampoo that could make me like my girl any less. But if you'll unwrap that package you may see why you had me going a while at first."

White fingers and nimble tore at the string and paper. And then an ecstatic scream of joy; and then, alas! a quick feminine change to hysterical tears and wails, necessitating the immediate employment of all the comforting powers of the lord of the flat.

 For there lay The Combs — the set of combs, side and back, that Della had worshipped for long in a Broadway window. Beautiful combs, pure tortoise shell, with jeweled rims — just the shade to wear in the beautiful vanished hair. They were expensive combs, she knew, and her heart had simply craved

and yearned over them without the least hope of possession. And now, they were hers, but the tresses that should have adorned the coveted adornments were gone.

But she hugged them to her bosom, and at length she was able to look up with dim eyes and a smile and say: "My hair grows so fast, Jim!"

And then Della leaped up like a little singed cat and cried, "Oh, oh!"

Jim had not yet seen his beautiful present. She held it out to him eagerly upon her open palm. The dull precious metal seemed to flash with a reflection of her bright and ardent spirit.

"Isn't it a dandy, Jim? I hunted all over town to find it. You'll have to look at the time a hundred times a day now. Give me your watch. I want to see how it looks on it."

Instead of obeying, Jim tumbled down on the couch and put his hands under the back of his head and smiled.

"Dell," said he, "let's put our Christmas presents away and keep 'em a while. They're too nice to use just at present. I sold the watch to get the money to buy your combs. And now suppose you put the chops on."

The magi, as you know, were wise men — wonderfully wise men who brought gifts to the Babe in the manger. They invented the art of giving Christmas presents. Being wise, their gifts were no doubt wise ones, possibly bearing the privilege of exchange in case of duplication. And here I have lamely related to you the uneventful chronicle of two foolish children in a flat who most unwisely sacrificed for each other the greatest treasures of their house. But in a last word to the wise of these days let it be said that of all who give gifts these two were the wisest. Of all who give and receive gifts, such as they are wisest. Everywhere they are wisest. They are the magi.

EUGENE FIELD

The First Christmas Tree

Once upon a time the forest was in a great commotion. Early in the evening the wise old cedars had shaken their heads ominously and predicted strange things. They had lived in the forest many, many years; but never had they seen such marvellous sights as were to be seen now in the sky, and upon the hills, and in the distant village.

"Pray tell us what you see," pleaded a little vine; "we who are not as tall as you can behold none of these wonderful things. Describe them to us, that we may enjoy them with you."

"I am filled with such amazement," said one of the cedars, "that I can hardly speak. The whole sky seems to be aflame, and the stars appear to be dancing among the clouds; angels walk down from heaven to the earth, and enter the village or talk with the shepherds upon the hills."

The vine listened in mute astonishment. Such things never before had happened. The vine trembled with excitement. Its nearest neighbor was a tiny tree, so small it scarcely ever was noticed; yet it was a very beautiful little tree, and the vines and ferns and mosses and other humble residents of the forest loved it dearly.

"How I should like to see the angels!" sighed the little tree, "and how I should like to see the stars dancing among the clouds! It must be very beautiful."

As the vine and the little tree talked of these things, the cedars watched with increasing interest the wonderful scenes over and beyond the confines of the forest. Presently they thought they heard music, and they were not mistaken, for soon the whole air was full of the sweetest harmonies ever heard upon earth.

"What beautiful music!" cried the little tree. "I wonder whence it comes."

"The angels are singing," said a cedar; "for none but angels could make such sweet music."

"But the stars are singing, too," said another cedar; "yes, and the shepherds on the hill join in the song, and what a strangely glorious song it is!"

The trees listened to the singing, but they did not understand its meaning: it seemed to be an anthem, and it was of a Child who had been born; but further than this they did not understand. The strange and glorious song continued all the night; and all that night the angels walked to and fro, and the shepherd-folk talked with the angels, and the stars danced and carolled in high heaven. And it was nearly morning when the cedars cried out, "They are coming to the forest! the angels are coming to the forest!" And, surely enough, this was true. The vine and the little tree were very terrified, and they begged their older and stronger neighbors to protect them from harm. But the cedars were too busy with their own fears to pay any heed to the faint pleadings of the humble vine and the little tree.

The angels came into the forest, singing the same glorious anthem about the Child, and the stars sang in chorus with them, until every part of the woods rang with echoes of that wondrous song. There was nothing in the appearance of this angel host to inspire fear; they were clad all in white, and there were crowns upon their fair heads, and golden harps in their hands; love, hope, charity, compassion, and joy beamed from their beautiful faces, and their presence seemed to fill the forest with a divine peace. The angels came through the forest to where the little tree stood, and gathering around it, they touched it with their hands, and kissed its little branches, and sang even more sweetly than before. And their song was about the Child, the Child, the Child who had been born. Then the stars came down from the skies and danced and hung upon the branches of the tree, and they, too, sang that song — the song of the Child. And all the other trees and the vines and the ferns and the mosses beheld in wonder; nor could they understand why all these things were being done, and why this exceeding honor should be shown the little tree.

When the morning came the angels left the forest — all but one angel, who remained behind and lingered near the little tree. Then a cedar asked: "Why do you tarry with us, holy angel?" And the angel answered: "I stay to guard this little tree, for it is sacred, and no harm shall come to it."

The little tree felt quite relieved by this assurance, and it held up its head more confidently than ever before. And how it thrived and grew, and waxed in strength and beauty! The cedars said they never had seen the like. The sun seemed to lavish its choicest rays upon the little tree, heaven dropped its sweetest dew upon it, and the winds never came to the forest that they did not forget their rude manners and linger to kiss the little tree and sing it their prettiest songs. No danger ever menaced it, no harm threatened; for the angel never slept — through the day and through the night the angel watched the little tree and protected it from all evil. Oftentimes the trees talked with the angel; but of course they understood little of what he said, for he spoke always of the Child who was to become the Master; and always when thus he talked, he caressed the little tree, and stroked its branches and leaves, and moistened them with his tears. It all was so very strange that none in the forest could understand.

So the years passed, the angel watching his blooming charge. Sometimes the beasts strayed toward the little tree and threatened to devour its tender foliage; sometimes the woodman came with his axe, intent upon hewing down the straight and comely thing; sometimes the hot, consuming breath of drought swept from the south, and sought to blight the forest and all its verdure: the angel kept them from the little tree. Serene and beautiful it grew, until now it was no longer a little tree, but the pride and glory of the forest.

One day the tree heard someone coming through the forest. Hitherto the angel had hastened to its side when men approached; but now the angel strode away and stood under the cedars yonder.

"Dear angel," cried the tree, "can you not hear the footsteps of someone approaching? Why do you leave me?"

"Have no fear," said the angel; "for he who comes is the Master."

The Master came to the tree and beheld it. He placed his hands upon its smooth trunk and branches, and the tree was thrilled with a strange and glorious delight. Then he stooped and kissed the tree, and then he turned and went away.

Many times after that the Master came to the forest, and when he came it always was to where the tree stood. Many times he rested beneath the tree and enjoyed the shade of its foliage, and listened to the music of the wind as it swept through the rustling leaves. Many times he slept there, and the tree watched over him, and the forest was still, and all its voices were hushed. And the angel hovered near like a faithful sentinel.

Ever and anon men came with the Master to the forest, and sat with him in the shade of the tree, and talked with him of matters which the tree never could understand; only it heard that the talk was of love and charity and gentleness, and it saw that the Master was beloved and venerated by the others. It heard them tell of the Master's goodness and humility — how he had healed the sick and raised the dead and bestowed inestimable blessings wherever he walked. And the tree loved the Master for his beauty and his goodness; and when he came to the forest it was full of joy, but when he came not it was sad. And the other trees of the forest joined in its happiness and its sorrow, for they, too, loved the Master. And the angel always hovered near.

The Master came one night alone into the forest, and his face was pale with anguish and wet with tears, and he fell upon his knees and prayed. The tree heard him, and all the forest was still, as if it were standing in the presence of death. And when the morning came, lo! the angel had gone.

Then there was a great confusion in the forest. There was a sound of rude voices, and a clashing of swords and staves. Strange men appeared, uttering loud oaths and cruel threats, and the tree was filled with terror. It called aloud for the angel, but the angel came not.

"Alas," cried the vine, "they have come to destroy the tree, the pride and glory of the forest!"

The forest was sorely agitated, but it was in vain. The strange men plied their axes with cruel vigor, and the tree was hewn to the ground. Its beautiful branches were cut away and cast aside, and its soft, thick foliage was strewn to the tenderer mercies of the winds.

"They are killing me!" cried the tree; "why is not the angel here to protect me?"

But no one heard the piteous cry — none but the other trees of the forest, and they wept, and the little vine wept too.

Then the cruel men dragged the despoiled and hewn tree from the forest; and the forest saw that beauteous thing no more.

But the night wind that swept down from the City of the Great King that night to ruffle the bosom of distant Galilee, tarried in the forest awhile to say that it had seen that day a cross upraised on Calvary — the tree on which was stretched the body of the dying Master.

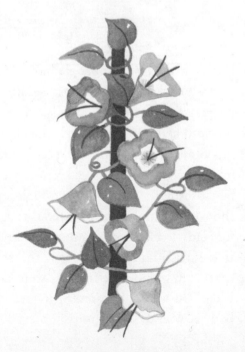

MARK TWAIN

Christmas at the Clemens' household must have been quite an exciting adventure!
Mark Twain (Samuel Langhorne Clemens) wrote this letter to his daughter, detailing
Santa's very specific instructions to fulfill her Christmas wishes.

Susie's Letter from Santa

Palace of Nicholas
In the Moon
Christmas Morning

My dear Susie Clemens:
I have received and read all the letters which you and your little sister have written me by the hand of your mother and your nurses; I have also read those which you little people have written me with your own hands — for although you did not use any characters that are in grown people's alphabet, you used the characters that all children in all lands on earth and in the twinkling stars use; and as all my subjects in the moon are children and use no characters but that, you will easily understand that I can read your and your baby sister's jagged and fantastic marks without any trouble at all. But I had trouble with those letters which you dictated through your mother and the nurses, for I am a foreigner and cannot read English writing well. You will find that I made no mistakes about the things which you and the baby ordered in your own letters — I went down your chimney at midnight when you were asleep and delivered them all myself — and kissed both of you, too, because you are good children, well trained, nice

mannered, and about the most obedient little people I ever saw. But in the letter which you dictated there were some words which I could not make out for certain, and one or two small orders which I could not fill because we ran out of stock. Our last lot of kitchen furniture for dolls has just gone to a very poor little child in the North Star away up in the cold country above the Big Dipper. Your mama can show you that star and country above the Big Dipper. Your mama can show you that star and you will say: "Little Snow Flake" (for that is the child's name), "I'm glad you got that furniture, for you need it more than I." That is, you must *write* that, with your own hand, and Snow Flake will write you an answer. If you only spoke it she wouldn't hear you. Make your letter light and thin, for the distance is great and postage very heavy.

There was a word or two in your mama's letter which I couldn't be certain of. I took it to be "a trunk full of doll's clothes." Is that it? I will call at your kitchen door about nine o'clock this morning to inquire. But I must not see anybody and I must not speak to anybody but you. When the kitchen doorbell rings, George must be blindfolded and sent to open the door. Then he must go back to the dining room or the china closet and take the cook with him. You must tell George he must walk on tiptoe and not speak — otherwise he will die someday. Then you must go up to the nursery and stand on a chair or the nurse's bed and put your ear to the speaking tube that leads down to the kitchen and when I whistle through it you must speak in the tube and say, "Welcome, Santa Claus!" Then I will ask whether it was a trunk you ordered or not. If you say it was, I shall ask you what *color* you want the trunk to be. Your mama will help you to name a nice color and then you must tell me every single thing in detail which you want the trunk to contain. Then when I say "Good-bye and a merry Christmas to my little Susie Clemens," you must say "Good-bye, good old Santa Claus, I thank you very much and please tell that little Snow Flake I will look at her star tonight and she must look down here — I will be right in the west bay window; and every fine night I will look at her star and say, 'I know somebody up there and *like* her, too.' " Then you must go down into the library and make George close the doors that open into the main hall and everybody must keep still for a little while. Then while you are waiting I will go to the moon and get those things and in a few minutes I will come down the chimney that belongs to the fireplace that is in the hall — if it is a trunk you want — because I couldn't get such a large thing as a trunk down the nursery chimney, you know.

People may talk if they want, till they hear my footsteps in the hall. Then you tell them to keep quiet a little while until I go up the chimney. Maybe you will not hear my footsteps at all — so you may go now and then and peep through the dining-room doors, and by and by you will see that which you want, right under the piano in the drawing room — for I shall put it there. If I should leave any snow in the hall, you must tell George to sweep it into the fireplace, for I haven't time to do such things. George must not use a broom, but a rag — or he will die someday. You watch George and don't let him run into danger. If my boot should leave a stain on the marble, George must not holystone it away. Leave it there always in memory of my visit; and whenever you look at it or show it to anybody you must let it remind you to be a good little girl. Whenever you are naughty and somebody points to that mark which your good old Santa Claus's boot made on the marble, what will you say, little sweetheart?

Good-bye for a few minutes, till I come down and ring the kitchen doorbell.

Your loving Santa Claus
Whom people sometimes call
"The Man in the Moon"

Christmas at the Cratchits'

Then up rose Mrs. Cratchit, Cratchit's wife, dressed out but poorly in a twice-turned gown, but brave in ribbons, which are cheap and make a goodly show for sixpence; and she laid the cloth, assisted by Belinda Cratchit, second of her daughters, also brave in ribbons; while Master Peter Cratchit plunged a fork into the saucepan of potatoes, and getting the corners of his monstrous shirt collar (Bob's private property, conferred upon his son and heir in honour of the day) into his mouth, rejoiced to find himself so gallantly attired, and yearned to show his linen in the fashionable Parks. And now two smaller Cratchits, boy and girl, came tearing in, screaming that outside the baker's they had smelt the goose, and known it for their own; and basking in luxurious thoughts of sage and onion, these young Cratchits danced about the table, and exalted Master Peter Cratchit to the skies, while he (not proud, although his collars nearly choked him) blew the fire, until the slow potatoes bubbling up, knocked loudly at the saucepan lid to be let out and peeled.

"What has ever got your precious father?" said Mrs. Cratchit. "And your brother, Tiny Tim! And Martha warn't as late last Christmas Day by half-an-hour!"

"Here's Martha, Mother!" said a girl, appearing as she spoke.

"Here's Martha, Mother!" cried the two young Cratchits. "Hurrah! There's *such* a goose, Martha!"

"Why, bless your heart alive, my dear, how late you are!" said Mrs. Cratchit, kissing her a dozen times, and taking off her shawl and bonnet for her with officious zeal.

"We'd a deal of work to finish up last night," replied the girl, "and had to clear away this morning, Mother!"

"Well! Never mind so long as you are come," said Mrs. Cratchit. "Sit ye down before the fire, my dear, and have a warm, Lord bless ye!"

"No, no! There's Father coming!" cried the two young Cratchits, who were everywhere at once. "Hide, Martha, hide!"

So Martha hid herself, and in came little Bob, the father, with at least three feet of comforter exclusive of the fringe, hanging down before him; and his threadbare clothes darned up and brushed, to look seasonable; and Tiny Tim upon his shoulder. Alas for Tiny Tim, he bore a little crutch, and had his limbs supported by an iron frame!

"Why, where's our Martha?" cried Bob Cratchit, looking round.

"Not coming," said Mrs. Cratchit.

"Not coming!" said Bob, with a sudden declension in his high spirits; for he had been Tim's blood horse all the way from church, and had come home rampant. "Not coming upon Christmas Day!"

Martha didn't like to see him disappointed, if it were only in joke; so she came out prematurely from behind the closet door, and ran into his arms, while the two young Cratchits hustled Tiny Tim, and bore him off into the wash-house, that he might hear the pudding singing in the copper.

"And how did little Tim behave?" asked Mrs. Cratchit, when she had rallied Bob on his credulity, and Bob had hugged his daughter to his heart's content.

"As good as gold," said Bob, "and better. Somehow he gets thoughtful, sitting by himself so much, and thinks the strangest things you ever heard. He told me, coming home, that he hoped the people saw him in the church, because he was a cripple, and it might be pleasant to them to remember upon Christmas Day, who made lame beggars walk and blind men see."

Bob's voice was tremulous when he told them this, and trembled more when he said that Tiny Tim was growing strong and hearty.

His active little crutch was heard upon the floor, and back came Tiny Tim before another word was spoken, escorted by his brother and sister to his stool before the fire; and while Bob, turning up his cuffs — as if, poor fellow, they were capable of being made more shabby — compounded some hot mixture in a jug with gin and lemons, and stirred it round and round and put it on the hob to simmer, Master Peter and the two ubiquitous young Cratchits went to fetch the goose, with which they soon returned in high procession.

Such a bustle ensued that you might have thought a goose the rarest of all birds; a feathered phenomenon, to which a black swan was a matter of course, and in truth it was something very like it in that house. Mrs. Cratchit made the gravy (ready beforehand in a little saucepan) hissing hot; Master Peter mashed the potatoes with incredible vigour; Miss Belinda sweetened up the apple sauce; Martha dusted the hot plates; Bob took Tiny Tim beside him in a tiny corner at the table; the two young Cratchits set chairs for everybody, not forgetting themselves, and mounting guard upon their posts, crammed spoons into their mouths, lest they should shriek for goose before their turn came to be helped. At last the dishes were set on, and grace was said. It was succeeded by a breathless pause, as Mrs. Cratchit, looking slowly all along the carving-knife, prepared to plunge it in the breast; but when she did, and when the long-expected gush of stuffing issued forth, one murmur of delight arose all around the board, and even Tiny Tim, excited by the two young Cratchits, beat on the table with the handle of his knife, and feebly cried Hurrah!

There never was such a goose. Bob said he didn't believe there ever was such a goose cooked. Its tenderness and flavour, size and cheapness, were the themes of universal admiration. Eked out by the applesauce and mashed potatoes, it was a sufficient dinner for the whole family; indeed as Mrs. Cratchit said with great delight (surveying one small atom of a bone upon the dish), they hadn't ate it all at last! Yet everyone had had enough, and the youngest Cratchits, in particular, were steeped in sage and onion to the eyebrows! But now, the plates being changed by Miss Belinda, Mrs. Cratchit left the room alone — too nervous to bear witnesses — to take the pudding up and bring it in.

Suppose it should not be done enough! Suppose it should break in turning out! Suppose somebody should have got over the wall of the backyard, and stolen it, while they were merry with the goose — a supposition at which the two young Cratchits became livid! All sorts of horrors were supposed.

Halloa! A great deal of steam! The pudding was out of the copper. A smell like a washing day! That was the cloth. A smell like an eating house and a pastry cook's next door to each other, with a laundress's next door to that! That was the pudding! In half a minute Mrs. Cratchit entered — flushed, but smiling proudly — with the pudding, like a speckled cannonball, so hard and firm, blazing in half of half a quartern of ignited brandy, and bedight with Christmas holly stuck into the top.

"Oh, a wonderful pudding!" Bob Cratchit said, and calmly too, that he regarded it as the greatest success achieved by Mrs. Cratchit since their marriage. Mrs. Cratchit said that now the weight was off her mind, she would confess she had had her doubts about the quantity of flour. Everybody had something to say about it, but nobody said or thought it was at all a small pudding for a large family. It would have been flat heresy to do so. Any Cratchit would have blushed to hint at such a thing.

At last the dinner was all done, the cloth was cleared, the hearth swept, and the fire made up. The compound in the jug being tasted, and considered perfect, apples and oranges were put upon the table, and a shovelful of chestnuts on the fire. Then all the Cratchit family drew round the hearth in what Bob Cratchit called a circle, meaning half a one; and at Bob Cratchit's elbow stood the family display of glass. Two tumblers, and a custard cup without a handle.

These held the hot stuff from the jug, however, as well as golden goblets would have done; and Bob served it out with beaming looks, while the chestnuts on the fire sputtered and cracked noisily. Then Bob proposed:

"A Merry Christmas to us all, my dears. God bless us!"

Which all the family re-echoed.

"God bless us every one!" said Tiny Tim, the last of all.

ROBERT PENGOLD

Harry the Singing Angel

Harry wasn't all *that* upset at the beginning. After all, he had been a singing angel last year, as opposed to a "hovering" angel. The hovering angels were only two and three years old. They didn't say a word. They just stood at the front and looked good. Singing angels were four, five, and six, and Harry was five years old — "mature for his age," he had heard people say.

It was far better to be a singing angel, Harry had concluded last year, since singing angels didn't have to wear those weird halos or fancy wings — the wings of the singing angels were part of the collar of the costume. And . . . the song was pretty simple to sing — not a bad song as songs go. "Hark, the herald angels sing, glory to the newborn king, peace on earth and mercy mild, God and sinner reconciled." He had the words down cold, although he still had a little question about just exactly what "mercy mild" was all about.

Harry's older brother, Billy, was eight years old, and he was going to be a shepherd — also for the second time. Both Harry and Billy had their costumes, which only needed to be lengthened a little at the sleeves and hem. Grandma had finished hemming them even before the first rehearsal.

Yep, it was looking like a pretty routine Christmas program. "No big deal," Harry told himself.

That is, until the announcement came — the announcement about who was going to play the part of Baby Jesus.

Harry was not amused. Somebody — somebody totally out of their minds, he concluded — had decided that Baby Jesus was going to be played by Baby Tommy. *His* Baby Tommy. Not an anonymous new baby in the church . . . or a new kid on the block . . . but the new kid in the crib in the room next to his room at his house. Baby Tommy, Harry's little brother.

It wasn't that Harry didn't like Baby Tommy, or even love him. At least he never could have admitted it. Mom would have had a fit.

Harry wasn't sure exactly *what* he felt. He knew that in the beginning he had been very excited about having a baby in the house. It was all he had talked about for months. Everybody had said he was taking Mom's pregnancy all in stride. A baby had been welcome news.

Harry had been sure that with the arrival of a new baby, he would no longer have to bear the title of "little brother." He finally was going to be somebody's "big brother" — and that had a pretty cool ring to it. Mom had assured him that he didn't have to give up his bed or his room — he didn't even have to share his room, at least for awhile, she said.

Dad had talked about how much fun it would be to have three kids instead of just two, and Harry could see some advantages in that, too. Maybe with a baby brother or sister around, *he* wouldn't always be blamed when something broke or something went wrong. He was certain he could out-run, out-argue, and out-yell any baby. It might be nice to have somebody to boss around . . . just like Billy bossed him around.

Of course there was always the possibility the baby would be a girl, but Harry didn't really like to think about that. As far as he was concerned, it was much cooler to be the big brother of a baby *brother* than to be the big brother of a baby sister.

All in all, it was no-o-o-o problem. Harry was excited about having a baby in the family. That is . . . until Baby Tommy actually showed up.

From the best Harry could tell, Baby Tommy appeared to have taken over.

When Baby Tommy cried . . . both Mom and Dad jumped. Mom didn't seem very patient with either Billy or Harry these days . . . but when Baby Tommy needed a diaper change or to be fed, Mom was all smiles and lovey-dovey. Dad didn't seem to have as much time to play ball as he did before Baby Tommy arrived . . . but he *always* seemed to find time when he got home to pick up Baby Tommy and cuddle *him*.

And . . . it was pretty amazing all the things Mom and Dad both expected Harry to do now. Why, they expected him to be able to dress himself *completely,* even to tying real shoelaces, and to put his own dirty clothes in the hamper, and to smooth out his bed before kindergarten started. He had never had to do any of those things before Baby Tommy arrived. And not only that, but he had to carry his own dishes to the kitchen sink from the table and worst of all, he had to sit in the MIDDLE of the backseat. There went the window view.

To top it all off, neither Mom nor Dad had been very amused when Harry had suggested that maybe — just *maybe* — they might be able to trade in Baby Tommy on a baby that cried a little less. It was only a suggestion — he didn't see why everybody got *that* upset. It certainly didn't seem to be worth a time out and no dessert.

No, all in all, Baby Tommy had been a much better "idea" than a reality. And now . . . to have Baby Tommy as the STAR of the Christmas program . . . to have Baby Tommy playing Baby Jesus . . . well that was just too much to ask, even of a singing angel.

Mom had insisted that Harry go to practices and walk through the motions. Dad had backed up her order with that "look" of his. *But,* Harry decided all on his own, *nobody could make him sing.*

He could even open his mouth and pretend to be singing "Hark the herald angels sing" . . . but he didn't have to make a sound.

"Glory to the newborn king?" Yeah, right. He wasn't about to call Baby Tommy a newborn king — Dad was already calling him a "little prince" and that was far enough in the line of royalty.

Nope . . . Harry may not be able to boycott the entire Christmas program, but he certainly didn't have to sing. Of that he was not only certain, but determined. It would be his little secret and that was that. No singing for Harry *this* year.

He almost gave in when Miss Martin came to talk to him about singing. Miss Martin was his kindergarten Sunday school teacher, and besides Mom and Aunt Carla, she was the prettiest and nicest woman Harry had ever met. He had even thought that he might like to marry her someday, maybe after first grade. Miss Martin told great Bible stories — why, she even made some of those people in the Bible seem *real*. He liked Daniel a lot. It *would* have been scary to be thrown into a lion's den. Miss Martin seemed to understand that. And it would have been pretty gross to be in the belly of a whale like Jonah — Miss Martin sometimes used words like *gross*. And he especially liked what Miss Martin had to say about Jesus, and about how He healed people and did miracles and all.

Perhaps the *very* best thing about Miss Martin, though, was that she treated Harry — why, as if he was at least six years old, maybe even seven. She always called him "Harold," which had a very grown-up ring to it as far as Harry was concerned. That was his real name, of course, Harold Reginald Loveless. (But don't tell anybody about that name Reginald.) His older brother was William Samuel Loveless . . . Billy for short. And Baby Tommy was really named Thomas — well, Thomas *something* Loveless. Harry didn't like it when most people called him Harold, but with Miss Martin it was OK.

Miss Martin had come to him, asking in a very nice voice, "Harold, do you have a sore throat?"

"No, Miss Martin," he had replied.

"Well, I've noticed you aren't singing. You have such a nice, strong voice for a boy, and you always sing in tune and know all the words. We really need you to sing out *strong*, Harold. We can't do this very well without you!"

Harry had just looked down. He really didn't want to give Miss Martin any reason to dislike him, but he was determined *not* to sing if Baby Tommy was going to be Baby Jesus.

"Is something the matter?" Miss Martin had asked.

"No, ma'am," Harry had said.

"Well," Miss Martin said, "I know you know the words and you know the tune, so I believe that when the time comes, you'll be the best singing angel up there."

Harry really was pretty sorry that Miss Martin was going to be disappointed. But this year, it just couldn't be helped. He had one more year of being a singing angel ahead of him, and she would just have to wait until then. He had no doubt he *could* be the best singing angel. . . but not this year.

The days passed. Rehearsals came and went. Harry hoped against hope that another baby would be born or somebody else would be chosen to be Baby Jesus. He had even hoped in secret that Baby Tommy would get sick so they'd *have* to find another Baby Jesus. No such luck.

If anything, as the days went by, Tommy just got more and more attention, and became more and more demanding. Why, they even had a party for Baby Tommy and he got all kinds of gifts — it wasn't even Christmas or his birthday or *anything*. And it seemed everybody in the whole world had been by the house to oooh and aaah over Baby Tommy. They didn't even seem to notice Harry most of the time. It wasn't fair.

Certainly nothing had happened to change Harry's mind. He was determined more than ever to carry out his plan, even if nobody ever knew about it. He'd know, and that's all that mattered. There would be no singing from Harry Loveless' lips this year.

The evening of the Christmas program finally showed up, and so did Baby Tommy bundled in a soft white blanket. Mom helped Billy with the headdress he had to wear as a shepherd and she helped Harry into his singing-angel costume, but mostly she fussed over Baby Tommy, trying to put him to sleep before the show. Harry had to agree that he'd be a lot less trouble asleep than awake.

Miss Martin got everybody lined up in the right order. Then, Reverend Brown showed up to say a prayer and to tell all the angels, "Be sure to sing your best!" Harry pretended not to hear him, which wasn't really all that hard since Clarence Fosdick kept punching him in the ribs. (Even though he was also five years old, it was Clarence's first year as a singing angel and he seemed pretty nervous about it as best Harry could tell.)

Harry walked in like the pro that he was, and when he got up into the choir area, he took his place near the manger. All the kids did pretty good jobs in their speaking parts, he thought — the narrators telling the first part of the story while Mary and Joseph made their way to the choir from the back of the church. Mary was riding a REAL donkey this year! That was a new twist. Harry was pretty impressed and everybody else seemed to feel the same way. Yeah, this was turning out to be a pretty awesome Christmas program.

The innkeeper did his part and then Mary and Joseph sang a song and while the spotlight was just on them, a lady dressed all in black brought in Baby Tommy and put him in the manger.

"Baby Jesus, yeah right," Harry said under his breath. He was glad Baby Tommy seemed sound asleep. "He'll never even know he was Baby Jesus," Harry whispered to himself. "And maybe nobody else will."

Then the spotlight went away and the lights came up and Mary and Joseph went over and stood by the manger and Mary kneeled down and started to sing a little lullaby. To Harry's great surprise, she reached over and picked up Baby Jesus — that is, Baby Tommy. *Big mistake*, Harry thought to himself. *She's gonna wake him up!*

And sure enough, Baby Tommy started to whimper. Just a little at first. And then a little more.

Oh no! thought Harry. *He's going to spoil the whole thing.*

Harry glanced out at Mom and Dad on the second row and he could tell Mom was getting nervous. Dad, too. Billy was at the back of the church waiting to walk in with the shepherds. Harry could tell Baby Tommy was getting ready to wind up with one of his walloping cries — his face was scrunching up for that moment by moment. *What should he do?*

Then Baby Tommy really let loose with a cry. It was huge. In fact, it may have been the biggest baby cry that anybody had ever heard in that church. Harry could see the lady dressed in black start toward the back entrance to the choir area. *No!* Harry thought. *You can't have a Christmas program without a Baby Jesus in the manger. It just wouldn't be right. She can't come and take Baby Jesus away.*

Harry had known all along that Baby Tommy wasn't going to be a very good Baby Jesus, but Harry couldn't let Baby Tommy ruin the whole program. He stepped out of line without a glance at Miss Martin — he figured she'd probably be upset with him but it couldn't be helped. He quickly walked over and knelt down by the manger and stuck out his hand to take Baby Tommy's little fingers.

"It's OK," he said in a very low little voice while Mary went right on with her song. Baby Tommy seemed surprised at another touch and opened his eyes and Harry leaned over and patted him on the head and whispered, "It's OK. It's OK."

For a few seconds, Baby Tommy stopped whimpering as he seemed to stare up at Harry. Then Harry could see a cry starting to brew again.

Behind him, Harry heard the introduction from the organ for the singing angels song. *Maybe the music will keep him quiet,* Harry thought. But that cry still seemed on the way. *What could he do?* He had to do something! It wasn't at all what he had planned. But out of Harry's own mouth, he heard a song, "Hark, the herald angels sing" — Baby Tommy seemed to be listening!

Was that a smile? Harry wondered. He wasn't sure he'd ever seen Baby Tommy smile before. "Glory to the newborn king." Yep. Baby Tommy definitely seemed to be listening. "Peace on earth and mercy mild" — Now Baby Tommy was staring all around . . . "God and sinner reconciled."

Baby Tommy was closing his eyes! *Yeah, that's it.* Harry thought. And Mary, smart woman at last, put Baby Jesus — Baby Tommy, that is — back in the manger. Harry still held onto his hand, though, just in case. "Joyful all ye nations rise. Join the triumph in the skies" . . . Sure enough, Baby Tommy seemed to be going back to sleep. "With angelic hosts proclaim, Christ is born in Bethlehem." Harry could feel Baby Tommy's fingers loosening their grip so he let go and stood up to

rejoin the choir for the last line. After all he'd sung this much —
"Hark, the herald angels sing, glory to the newborn king."

Harry wasn't sure how the rest of the program turned out. He was
too busy watching Baby Jesus — that is, Baby Tommy. He guessed that
the shepherds did their part OK. Billy didn't say anything later and
neither did Mom or Dad so it must have gone alright. The wise men
were a big hit. They didn't come in riding on live camels, but they did
have humongous trains on their robes that had the entire audience
whispering. All Harry cared about was that Baby Tommy was asleep
and that he stayed asleep. Pretty soon it was over.

Backstage, everybody was in a jumble trying to get out of their
costumes and find their coats.

Harry was feeling very relieved, and then he saw Miss Martin
coming his way. *How could he tell her that he just had to get out of line?*
. . . but before he could get much further in his thinking, Miss Martin
gave him a big hug and then got down on his level so she could look
him right in the eye.

All she said was, "Hark! the angel Harold sang!"

Yeah, he guessed he had. "Well," Harry said to Miss Martin,
"sometimes you just have to help other people act like Jesus."

GRADY JOHNSON

How did outdoor Christmas lights become popular?
This 1953 magazine article traces their origin to the early 1900's.

𝔚hen Christmas 𝔚ent Outdoors

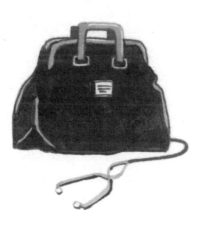

Thirty-five years ago this Christmas, ten-year-old David Jonathan Sturgeon lay in bed in Denver, doomed to die. To cheer him, his father lit a small Christmas tree in his sickroom.

Young David pointed through the window at an evergreen growing on the front lawn, exclaiming, "Oh, Daddy, please put some lights on that tree, too. It would look wonderful."

His father, David D. Sturgeon, operator of an electrical business, strung colored lights on the evergreen and David lay there smiling as he watched them sparkle like emeralds and rubies against their ermine mantle of snow.

The tree was the talk of the town. In horse-drawn carriages and chugging automobiles, people came from miles around to drive slowly past the Sturgeon home and admire the tree which Denverites proudly believe was the first lighted living Christmas tree in the land.

The Christmas after next, little David was dead. But neighbors, who had marveled at his tree, lit trees in their own yards and gardens, turning their section of town into a glittering fairyland. House by house, block by block, the idea spread; and through the years, more and more of these dazzling monuments to a dying boy's wish appeared.

Eight years later, in San Francisco, another little boy was sick at Christmastime. Because the lad couldn't see the family tree, Clarence F. "Sandy" Pratt painted some full-size light globes and strung them on a wire around an evergreen on his lawn across the street.

Like Denver's tree, it attracted much attention. And before New Year's Eve, the sick boy was well.

This so impressed Sandy Pratt that he resolved to spend the rest of his life persuading others not only to light living trees but to plant them. He organized the Outdoor Christmas Tree Association of California, and began sending two-year-old redwood seedlings to anyone who would promise to care for them and light them at Christmastime.

Today, in city parks, along highways, on dark and snow-drifted lawns alike, lighted living trees remind millions of the birth of Christ.

The beloved Little House on the Prairie *writer
shares one of her most vivid Christmas memories.*

Christmas When I Was Sixteen

DECEMBER 1924

The snow was scudding low over the drifts of the white world outside the little claim shanty. It was blowing through the cracks in its walls and forming little piles and miniature drifts on the floor, and even on the desks before which several children sat, trying to study; for this abandoned claim shanty, which had served as the summer home of a homesteader on the Dakota prairie, was being used as a schoolhouse during the winter.

The walls were made of one thickness of wide boards with cracks between and the enormous stove that stood nearly in the center of the one room could scarcely keep out the frost, though its sides were a glowing red. The children were dressed warmly and had been allowed to gather closely around the stove following the advice of the county superintendent of schools who, on a recent visit, had said that the only thing he had to say to them was to keep their feet warm.

This was my first school; I'll not say how many years ago, but I was only sixteen years old and twelve miles from home during a frontier winter. I walked a mile over the unbroken snow from my boarding place to school every morning and back at night. There were only a few pupils, and on this particular snowy afternoon, they were restless, for it was nearing 4 o'clock and tomorrow was Christmas. "Teacher" was restless too though she tried not to show it, for she was wondering if she could get home for Christmas Day.

It was almost too cold to hope for Father to come, and a storm was hanging in the northwest which might mean a blizzard at any minute. Still, tomorrow was Christmas — and then there was a jingle of sleigh bells outside. A man in a huge fur coat in a sleigh full of robes passed the window. I was going home after all!

When one thinks of twelve miles now, it is in terms of motor cars and means only a few minutes. It was different then, and I'll never forget that ride. The bells made a merry jingle, and the fur robes were warm; but the weather was growing colder, and the snow was drifting so that the horses must break their way through the drifts.

We were facing the strong wind, and every little while he, who later became the "Man of the Place," must stop the team, get out in the snow, and by putting his hands over each horse's nose in turn, thaw the ice from them where the breath had frozen over their nostrils. Then he would get back into the sleigh, and on we'd go until once more the horses could not breathe for the ice.

When we reached the journey's end, it was 40 degrees below zero; the snow was blowing so thickly that we could not see across the street; and I was so chilled that I had to be half carried into the house. But I was home for Christmas, and cold and danger were forgotten.

Such magic there is in Christmas to draw the absent ones home, and if unable to go in the body, the thoughts will hover there! Our hearts grow tender with childhood memories and love of kindred, and we are better throughout the year for having, in spirit, become a child again at Christmastime.

Santa Claus and St. Nicholas

 anta Claus, Saint Nick, Father Christmas, Bonhomme Noel, Knecht Clobes, or whatever else a child may call the kind old gentleman who comes with a sack of toys and goodies at Christmas time — the fact is, he is a legendary memory of a real person named Nicholas.

Saint Nicholas, whose feast day is celebrated December 6, lived in the fourth century. His parents died when he was a young man, leaving him financially well off. Nicholas decided to use his inheritance for works of charity. Nicholas became a legend in his own area, and was soon synonymous with any person who went about doing generous acts in secret.

After he had given away all of his money, Nicholas entered a monastery as a monk, and was later named a bishop in the church. All over the world, this tradition of Nicholas' kindness and generosity has become associated with Christmas.

In France, Santa Claus is called Bonhomme Noel. He is accompanied by a thin, weasel-faced old man with a long gray beard and threatening dark eyes: Le Pere Fouettard, or "Father Whipper." Father Whipper carries on his shoulder a wickerwork basket filled with tiny birch rods, and he leaves one of these whips for every child who has been naughty, cross, or greedy during the year. Father Christmas, of course, comes only to children who are trying to be good. In other cultures, children who are naughty find a lump of coal in their stockings or wooden shoes.

Saint Nicholas often appears in churches and Sunday schools on December 6 to give "gold coin" chocolates to children. He is especially popular in Europe.

Children in Holland leave hay and carrots with dishes of water on their windowsills for St. Nick's white pony. Syrian children leave bowls of water and wheat outside their houses for the camels of the wise men (who are thought to bring them gifts). Good boys and girls find gifts on Christmas morning, but naughty ones find black marks on their wrists. Children in Belgium leave wooden shoes with food in them for Father Christmas' reindeer.

Santa Claus is the version of St. Nicholas known to children in the United States. Santa and Mrs. Claus live at the North Pole, where elves employed by the Claus's create toys throughout the year for delivery to children on Christmas Eve. These toys are delivered by Santa Claus in a flying sleigh pulled by nine reindeer. Santa delivers toys to each home by dropping through chimneys and stove pipes. He — or one of his helpers — often can be seen taking requests for toys prior to Christmas.

Like many traditions and legends, the stories of Saint Nicholas and Santa Claus continue to be enhanced and altered. One constant, however, has remained through the centuries: secret giving from a generous heart.

— Essay by Jan Dargatz

CHRISTOPHER MORLEY

The Tree That Didn't Get Trimmed

If you walk through a grove of balsam trees you will notice that the young trees are silent; they are listening. But the old tall ones — especially the firs — are whispering. They are telling the story of The Tree That Didn't Get Trimmed. It sounds like a painful story, and the murmur of the old trees as they tell it is rather solemn; but it is an encouraging story for young saplings to hear. . . .

All young fir trees dream of being a Christmas Tree some day. With the vision of that brightness and gaiety before them they patiently endure the sharp sting of the ax, the long hours pressed together on a freight car. But every December there are more trees cut down than are needed for Christmas. And that is the story that no one . . . has thought to put down.

The tree in this story should never have been cut. He wouldn't have been, but it was getting dark in the Vermont woods, and the man with the ax said to himself, "Just one more."

The tree was a fine, well-grown youngster, but too tall for his age; his branches were rather scraggly. If he'd been left there he would have been an unusually big tree some day; but now he was in the awkward age and didn't have the tapering shape and the thick, even foliage that people like on Christmas trees. Worse still, instead of running up to a straight, clean spire, his top was a bit lopsided, with a fork in it.

But he didn't know this as he stood with many others, leaning against the side wall of the green grocer's shop. In those cold December days he was very happy, thinking of the pleasures to come. He had heard of the delights of Christmas Eve: the stealthy setting-up of the tree, the tinsel balls and the colored toys and stars, the peppermint canes and birds with spun-glass tails. Even that old anxiety of Christmas trees — burning candles — did not worry him, for he had been told that nowadays people used strings of tiny electric bulbs which cannot set one on fire. So he looked forward to the festival with a confident heart.

"I shall be very grand," he said. "I hope there will be children to admire me. It must be a great moment when the children hang their stockings on you!" He even felt sorry for the first trees that were chosen and taken away. It would be best, he considered, not to be bought until Christmas Eve. Then, in the shining darkness someone would pick him out, put him carefully along the running board of a car, and away they would go. The tire chains would clack and jingle merrily on the snowy road. He imagined a big house with fire glowing on a hearth; the hushed rustle of wrapping paper and parcels being unpacked. Someone would say, "Oh, what a beautiful tree!" How erect and stiff he would brace himself in his iron tripod stand.

But day after day went by, one by one the other trees were taken, and he began to grow troubled. For everyone who looked at him seemed to have an unkind word. "Too tall," said one lady. "No, this one wouldn't do, the branches are too skimpy," said another. "If I chop off the top," said the green grocer, "it wouldn't be so bad." The tree shuddered, but the customer had already passed on to look at others. Some of his branches ached where the grocer had bent them upward to make his shape more attractive.

Then he was shown to a lady who wanted a tree very cheap. "You can have this one for a dollar," said the grocer. This was only one-third of what the grocer had asked for him at first, but even so the lady refused him and went across the street to buy a little artificial tree at the toy store. The man pushed him back carelessly, and he toppled over and fell alongside the wall. No one bothered to pick him up. He was almost glad, for now his pride would be spared.

Now it was Christmas Eve. It was a foggy evening with a drizzling rain; the alley alongside the store was thick with trampled slush. As he lay there among broken boxes and fallen scraps of holly strange thoughts came to him. He remembered the wintry sparkle of the woods, the big trees with crusts and clumps of silver on their broad boughs, the keen singing of the lonely wind. He remembered the strong, warm feeling of his roots reaching down into the safe earth. That was such a good feeling; it means to a tree just what it means to you to stretch your toes down toward the bottom of a well-tucked bed. And he had given up all this to lie here, disdained and forgotten, in a littered alley. The splash of feet, the chime of bells, the cry of cars went past him. He trembled a little with self-pity and vexation. "No toys and stockings for me," he thought sadly, and shed some of his needles.

Late that night, after all the shopping was over, the grocer came out to clear away what was left. The boxes, the broken wreaths, the empty barrels, and our tree with one or two others that hadn't been sold, all were thrown through the side door into the cellar. The door was locked and he lay there in the dark. One of his branches, doubled under him in the fall, ached so he thought it must be broken. "So this is Christmas," he said to himself.

All that day it was very still in the cellar. There was an occasional creak as one of the bruised trees tried to stretch itself. Feet went along the pavement overhead, and there was a booming of church bells, but everything had a slow, disappointed sound. Christmas is always a little sad, after such busy preparations. The unwanted trees lay on the stone floor, watching the furnace light flicker on a hatchet that had been left there.

The day after Christmas a man came in who wanted some green boughs to decorate a cemetery. The grocer took the hatchet, and seized the trees without ceremony. They were too disheartened to care. Chop, chop, chop, went the blade, and the sweet-smelling branches were carried away. The naked trunks were thrown into a corner.

And now our tree, what was left of him, had plenty of time to think. He no longer could feel anything, for trees feel with their branches, but they think with their trunks. What did he think about as he grew dry and stiff? He thought that it had been silly of him to imagine such a fine, gay career for himself, and he was sorry for the other young trees, still growing in the fresh hilly country, who were enjoying the same fantastic dreams.

Now perhaps you don't know what happens to the trunks of leftover Christmas trees. You could never guess. Farmers come in from the suburbs and buy them at five cents each for beanpoles and grape arbors. So perhaps (here begins the encouraging part of his story) they are really happier, in the end, than the trees that get trimmed for Santa Claus. They go back into the fresh, moist earth of spring, and when the sun grows hot the quick tendrils of the vines climb up them and presently they are decorated with the red blossoms of the bean or the little blue globes of the grape, just as pretty as any Christmas trinkets.

So one day the naked, dusty fir poles were taken out of the cellar, and thrown into a trunk with many others, and made a rattling journey out into the land. The farmer unloaded them in his yard and was stacking them up by the barn when his wife came out to watch him.

"There!" she said. "That's just what I want, a nice long pole with a fork in it. Jim, put that one over there to hold up the clothesline." It was the first time that anyone had praised our tree, and his dried-up heart swelled with a tingle of forgotten sap. They put him near one end of the clothesline, with his stump close to a flower bed. The fork that had been despised for a Christmas tree was just the thing to hold up a clothesline. It was wash day, and soon the farmer's wife began bringing out wet garments to swing and freshen in the clean, bright air. And the very first thing that hung near the top of the Christmas pole was a cluster of children's stockings.

That isn't quite the end of the story, as the old fir trees whisper it in the breeze. The Tree That Didn't Get Trimmed was so cheerful watching the stockings, and other gay little clothes that plumped out in the wind . . . that he didn't notice what was going on — or going up — below him. A vine had caught hold of his trunk and was steadily twisting upward. And one morning, when the farmer's wife came out intending to shift him, she stopped and exclaimed. "Why, I mustn't move this pole," she said. "The morning glory has run right up it." So it had, and our bare pole was blue and crimson with color.

Something nice, the old firs believe, always happens to the trees that don't get trimmed.

What Christmas Is as We Grow Older

Time was, with most of us, when Christmas Day encircling all our limited world like a magic ring, left nothing out for us to miss or seek; bound together all our home enjoyments, affections, and hopes! Grouped everything and everyone around the Christmas fire; and made the little picture shining in our bright young eyes, complete.

Time came, perhaps, all too soon, when our thoughts overleaped that narrow boundary.

That was the time for the bright visionary Christmases which have long arisen from us to show faintly, after summer rain, in the palest edges of the rainbow! That was the time for the beatified enjoyment of the things that were to be, and never were, and yet the things that were so real in our resolute hope that it would be hard to say, now, what realities achieved since, have been stronger!

What! Is our life here, at the best, so constituted that, pausing as we advance at such a noticeable milestone in the track as this great birthday, we look back on the things that never were, as naturally and full, as gravely as on the things that have been and are gone, or have been and still are? If it be so, and so it seems to be, must we come to the conclusion that life is little better than a dream, and little worth the loves and strivings that we crowd into it?

No! Far be such miscalled philosophy from us, dear Reader, on Christmas Day! Nearer and closer to our hearts be the Christmas spirit, which is the spirit of active usefulness, perseverance, cheerful discharge of duty, kindness and forbearance! It is in the last virtues especially, that we are, or should be, strengthened by the unaccomplished visions of our youth; for, who shall say that they are not our teachers to deal gently even with the impalpable nothings of the earth!

Therefore, as we grow older, let us be more thankful that the circle of our Christmas associations and of the lessons that they bring, expands! Let us welcome every one of them, and summon them to take their places by the Christmas hearth.

Welcome, old aspirations, glittering creatures of an ardent fancy, to your shelter underneath the holly! We know you, and have not outlived you yet. Welcome, old projects and old loves, however fleeting, to your nooks among the steadier lights that burn around us. Welcome, all that was ever real to our hearts; and for the earnestness that made you real, thanks to heaven! Do we build no Christmas castles in the clouds now? Let our thoughts, fluttering like butterflies among these flowers of children, bear witness! Before this boy, there stretches out a Future, brighter than we ever looked on in our old romantic time, but bright with honor and with truth.

Welcome, everything! Welcome, alike what has been, and what never was, and what we hope may be, to your shelter underneath the holly, to your places round the Christmas fire, where what is sits openhearted! In yonder shadow, do we see obtruding furtively upon the blaze, an enemy's face? By Christmas Day we do forgive him! If the injury he has done us may admit of such companionship, let him come here and take his place. If otherwise, unhappily, let him go hence, assured that we will never injure nor accuse him.

On this day we shut out Nothing!

"Pause," says a low voice. "Nothing? Think!"

"On Christmas Day, we will shut out from our fireside, Nothing."

"Not the shadow of a vast City where the withered leaves are lying deep?" the voice replies. "Not the shadow that darkens the whole globe? Not the shadow of the City of the Dead?"

Not even that. Of all days in the year, we will turn our faces towards that City upon Christmas Day, and from its silent hosts bring those we loved, among us. City of the Dead, in the blessed name wherein we are gathered together at this time, and in the Presence that is here among us according to the promise, we will receive, and not dismiss, the people who are dear to us!

Yes. We can look upon these children angels that alight, so solemnly, so beautifully among the living children by the fire, and can bear to think how they departed from us. Entertaining angels unawares, as the Patriarchs did, the playful children are unconscious of their guests; but we can see them — can see a radiant arm around one favourite neck, as if there were a tempting of that child away.

There was a gallant boy, who fell, far away, upon a burning sand beneath a burning sun, and said, "Tell them at home, with my last love, how much I could have wished to kiss them once, but that I died contented and had done my duty!" Or there was another, over whom they read the words, "Therefore we commit his body to the deep," and so consigned him to the lonely ocean and sailed on. Or there was another, who lay down to his rest in the dark shadow of great forests, and, on earth, awoke no more. Oh shall they not, from sand and sea and forest, be brought home at such a time?

There was a dear girl — almost a woman — never to be one — who made a mourning Christmas in a house of joy, and went her trackless way to the silent City. We had a friend who was our friend from early days, with whom we often pictured the changes that were to come upon our lives, and merrily imagined how we would speak, and walk, and think, and talk, when we came to be old. His destined habitation in the City of the Dead received him in his prime. Shall he be shut out from our Christmas remembrance? Would his love have so excluded us?

Lost friend, lost child, lost parent, sister, brother, husband, wife, we will not so discard you! You shall hold your cherished places in our

Christmas hearts, and by our Christmas fires; and in the season of immortal hope, and on the birthday of immortal mercy, we will shut out Nothing!

The winter sun goes down over town and village; on the sea it makes a rosy path, as if the Sacred tread were fresh upon the water. A few more moments, and it sinks, and night comes on, and lights begin to sparkle in the prospect. On the hillside beyond the shapelessly-diffused town, and in the quiet keeping of the trees that gird the village steeple, remembrances are cut in stone, planted in common flowers, growing in grass, entwined with lowly brambles around many a mound of earth. In town and village, there are doors and windows closed against the weather, there are flaming logs heaped high, there are joyful faces, there is healthy music of voices. Be all ungentleness and harm excluded from the temples of the household . . . but be those remembrances admitted with tender encouragement. They are of the time and all its comforting and peaceful reassurances; and of the history that reunited even upon earth the living and the dead; and of the broad beneficence and goodness that too many men have tried to tear to narrow shreds.

The Elves and the Shoemaker

There was once a shoemaker who worked very hard and was very honest; but still he could not earn enough to live upon, and at last all he had in the world was gone, except just leather enough to make one pair of shoes. Then he cut them all ready to make up the next day, meaning to get up early in the morning to work. His conscience was clear and his heart light amidst all his troubles; so he went peaceably to bed, left all his cares to heaven, and fell asleep. In the morning, after he had said his prayers, he set himself down to his work, when, to his great wonder, there stood the shoes, already made, upon the table. The good man knew not what to say or think of this strange event. He looked at the workmanship; there was not one false stitch in the whole job; and all was so neat and true, that it was a complete masterpiece.

That same day a customer came in, and the shoes pleased him so well that he willingly paid a price higher than usual for them; and the poor shoemaker with the money bought leather enough to make two pairs more. In the evening he cut out the work, and went to bed early that he might get up and begin betimes next day: but he was saved all the trouble, for when he got up in the morning the work was finished ready to his hand. Presently in came buyers, who paid him handsomely for his goods, so that he bought leather enough for four pairs more. He cut out the work again overnight, and found it finished in the morning as before; and so it went on for some time: what was got ready in the evening was always done by daybreak, and the good man soon became thriving and prosperous again.

One evening about Christmastime, as he and his wife were sitting over the fire chatting together, he said to her, "I should like to sit up and watch tonight, that we may see who it is that comes and does my work for me." The wife liked the thought; so they left a light burning, and hid themselves in the corner of the room behind a curtain that was hung up there, and watched what should happen.

As soon as it was midnight, there came two little naked dwarfs; and they sat themselves upon the shoemaker's bench, took up all the work that was cut out, and began to ply with their little fingers, stitching and rapping and tapping away at such a rate, that the shoemaker was all amazement, and could not take his eyes off for a moment. And on they went till the job was quite finished, and the shoes stood ready for use upon the table. This was long before day-break; and then they bustled away as quick as lightning.

The next day the wife said to the shoemaker, "These little wights have made us rich, and we ought to be thankful to them, and do them a good office in return. I am quite vexed to see them run about as they do; they have nothing upon their backs to keep off the cold. I'll tell you what, I will make each of them a shirt, and a coat and waistcoat, and a pair of pantaloons into the bargain; you make each of them a little pair of shoes."

The thought pleased the good shoemaker very much; and one evening, when all the things were ready, they laid them on the table instead of the work that they used to cut out, and then went and hid themselves to watch what the little elves would do.

About midnight they came in, and were going to sit down to their work as usual; but when they saw the clothes lying for them, they laughed and were greatly delighted. Then they dressed themselves in the twinkling of an eye, and danced and capered and sprang about as merry as could be, till at last they danced out at the door over the green; and the shoemaker saw them no more: but everything went well with him from that time forward, as long as he lived.

HANS CHRISTIAN ANDERSEN

The Little Match Girl

It was late on a bitterly cold, snowy, New Year's Eve. A poor little girl was wandering in the dark cold streets; she was bareheaded and barefooted. She certainly had had shoes on when she left home, but they were not much good, for they were so huge. They had last been worn by her mother, and they fell off the poor little girl's feet when she was running across the street to avoid two carriages that were rolling rapidly by. One of the shoes could not be found at all; and the other was picked up by a boy, who ran off with it, saying that it would do for a cradle when he had children of his own. So the poor little girl had to go on with her little bare feet, which were blue with the cold. She carried a quantity of matches in her old apron, and held a packet of them in her hand. Nobody had bought any from her during all the long day; nobody had even given her a copper.

The poor little creature was hungry and perishing with cold, and she looked the picture of misery. The snowflakes fell upon her long yellow hair, which curled so prettily round her face, but she paid no attention to that. Lights were shining from every window, and there was a most delicious odor of roast goose in the streets, for it was New Year's Eve — she could not forget that. She found a protected place where one house projected a little beyond the next one, and here she crouched, drawing up her feet under her, but she was colder than ever. She did not dare go home, for she had not sold any matches and had not earned a single penny. Her father would beat her; besides, it was almost as cold at home as it was here. They lived in a house where the wind whistled through every crack, although they tried to stuff up the biggest ones with rags and straw. Her tiny hands were almost paralyzed with cold. Oh, if she could only find some way to warm them! Dared she pull one match out of the bundle and strike it on the wall to warm her fingers? She pulled one out. "Ritsch!" How it spluttered, how it blazed! It burnt with a bright clear flame, just like a little candle when she held her hand round it. It was a very curious candle, too. The little girl fancied that she was sitting in front of a big stove with polished brass feet and handles. There was a splendid fire blazing in it and warming her so beautifully, but — what happened? Just as she was stretching out her feet to warm them, the blaze went out, the stove vanished, and she was left sitting with the end of the burnt-out match in her hand. She struck a new one, it burnt, it blazed up, and where the light fell upon the wall against which she lay, it became transparent like gauze, and she could see right through it into the room inside. There was a table spread with a snowy cloth and pretty china; a roast goose stuffed with apples and prunes was steaming on it. And what was even better, the goose hopped from the dish with the carving knife and fork sticking in his back, and it waddled across the floor. It came right up to the poor child, and then — the match went out and there was nothing to be seen but the thick black wall.

She lit another match. This time she was sitting under a lovely Christmas tree. It was much bigger and more beautifully decorated than the one she had seen when she had peeped through the glass doors at the rich merchant's house this Christmas day. Thousands of lighted candles gleamed upon its branches, and coloured pictures such as she had seen in the shop windows looked down upon her. The little girl stretched out both her hands toward them — then out went the match. All the Christmas candles rose higher and higher, till she saw that they were only the twinkling stars. One of them fell and made a bright streak of light across the sky. "Someone is dying," thought the little girl; for her old grandmother, the only person who had ever been kind to her, used to say, "When a star falls a soul is going up to God."

Now she struck another match against the wall, and this time it was her grandmother who appeared in the circle of flame. She saw her quite clearly and distinctly, looking so gentle and happy.

"Grandmother!" cried the little creature. "Oh, do take me with you! I know you will vanish when the match goes out; you will vanish like the warm stove, the delicious goose, and the beautiful Christmas tree!"

She hastily struck a whole bundle of matches, because she did so want to keep her grandmother with her. The light of the matches made it as bright as day. Grandmother had never before looked so big or so beautiful. She lifted the little girl up in her arms, and they soared in a halo of light and joy, far, far above the earth, where there was no more cold, no hunger, no pain, for they were with God.

LIZZIE DEAS

The Christmas Rose

AN OLD LEGEND

WHEN the Magi laid their rich offerings of myrrh, frankincense, and gold, by the bed of the sleeping Christ Child, legend says that a shepherd maiden stood outside the door quietly weeping.

She, too, had sought the Christ Child. She, too, desired to bring him gifts. But she had nothing to offer, for she was very poor indeed. In vain she had searched the countryside over for one little flower to bring Him, but she could find neither bloom nor leaf, for the winter had been cold.

And as she stood there weeping, an angel passing saw her sorrow, and stooping he brushed aside the snow at her feet. And there sprang up on the spot a cluster of beautiful winter roses — waxen white with pink tipped petals.

"Nor myrrh, nor frankincense, nor gold," said the angel, "is offering more meet for the Christ Child than these pure Christmas roses."

Joyfully the shepherd maiden gathered the flowers and made her offering to the Holy Child.

LOUISA MAY ALCOTT

Christmas at Orchard House

Jo was the first to wake in the gray dawn of Christmas morning. No stockings hung at the fireplace, and for a moment she felt as much disappointed as she did long ago, when her little sock fell down because it was so crammed with goodies. Then she remembered her mother's promise, and, slipping her hand under her pillow, drew out a little crimson-covered book. She knew it very well, for it was that beautiful old story of the best life ever lived, and Jo felt that it was a true guidebook for any pilgrim going the long journey. She woke Meg with a "Merry Christmas," and bade her see what was under her pillow. A green-covered book appeared, with the same picture inside, and a few words written by their mother, which made their one present very precious in their eyes. Presently Beth and Amy woke, to rummage and find their little books also — one dove-colored, the other blue; and all sat looking at and talking about them, while the east grew rosy with the coming day. In spite of her small vanities, Margaret had a sweet and pious nature, which unconsciously influenced her sisters, especially Jo, who loved her very tenderly, and obeyed her because her advice was so gently given.

"Girls," said Meg seriously, looking from the tumbled head beside her to the two little night-capped ones in the room beyond, "Mother wants us to read and love and mind these books, and we must begin at once. We used to be faithful about it; but since father went away, and all this war trouble unsettled us, we have neglected many things. You can do as you please; but I shall keep my book on the table here, and read a little every morning as soon as I wake, for I know it will do me good, and help me through the day."

Then she opened her new book and began to read. Jo put her arm round her, and, leaning cheek to cheek, read also, with the quiet expression so seldom seen on her restless face.

"How good Meg is! Come, Amy, let's do as they do. I'll help you with the hard words, and they'll explain things if we don't understand," whispered Beth, very much impressed by the pretty books and her sisters' example.

"I'm glad mine is blue," said Amy; and then the rooms were very still while the pages were softly turned, and the winter sunshine crept in to touch the bright heads and serious faces with Christmas greeting.

"Where is mother?" asked Meg, as she and Jo ran down to thank her for their gifts, half an hour later.

"Goodness only knows. Some poor creeter come a-beggin', and your ma went straight off to see what was needed. There never was such a woman for givin' away vittles and drink, clothes and firin'," replied Hannah, who had lived with the family since Meg was born, and was considered by them all more as a friend than a servant.

"She will be back soon, I think; so fry your cakes, and have everything ready," said Meg, looking over the presents which were collected in a basket and kept under the sofa, ready to be produced at the proper time. "Why, where is Amy's bottle of cologne?" she added, as the little flask did not appear.

"She took it out a minute ago, and went off with it to put a ribbon on it, or some such notion," replied Jo, dancing about the room to take the first stiffness off the new army slippers.

"How nice my handkerchiefs look, don't they? Hannah washed and ironed them for me, and I marked them all myself," said Beth, looking proudly at the somewhat uneven letters which had cost her such labor.

"Bless the child! she's gone and put 'Mother' on them instead of 'M. March.' How funny!" cried Jo, taking up one.

"Isn't it right? I thought it was better to do it so, because Meg's initials are 'M.M.,' and I don't want anyone to use these but Marmee," said Beth, looking troubled.

"It's all right, dear, and a very pretty idea — quite sensible, too, for no one can ever mistake now. It will please her very much, I know," said Meg, with a frown for Jo and a smile for Beth.

"There's mother. Hide the basket, quick!" cried Jo, as a door slammed, and steps sounded in the hall.

Amy came in hastily, and looked rather abashed when she saw her sisters all waiting for her.

"Where have you been, and what are you hiding behind you?" asked Meg, surprised to see, by her hood and cloak, that lazy Amy had been out so early.

"Don't laugh at me, Jo! I didn't mean anyone should know till the time came. I only meant to change the little bottle for a big one, and I gave *all* my money to get it, and I'm truly trying not to be selfish anymore."

As she spoke, Amy showed the handsome flask which replaced the cheap one; and looked so earnest and humble in her little effort to forget herself that Meg hugged her on the spot, and Jo pronounced her "a trump," while Beth ran to the window, and picked her finest rose to ornament the stately bottle.

"You see I felt ashamed of my present, after reading and talking about being good this morning, so I ran round the corner and changed it the minute I was up: and I'm *so* glad, for mine is the handsomest now."

Another bang of the street door sent the basket under the sofa, and the girls to the table, eager for breakfast.

"Merry Christmas, Marmee! Many of them! Thank you for our books; we read some, and mean to every day," they cried, in chorus.

"Merry Christmas, little daughters! I'm glad you began at once, and hope you will keep on. But I want to say one word before we sit down. Not far away from here lies a poor woman with a little newborn baby. Six children are huddled into one bed to keep from freezing, for they have no fire. There is nothing to eat over there; and the oldest boy came to tell me they were suffering hunger and cold. My girls, will you give them your breakfast as a Christmas present?"

They were all unusually hungry, having waited nearly an hour, and for a minute no one spoke; only a minute, for Jo exclaimed impetuously, "I'm so glad you came before we began!"

"May I go and help carry the things to the poor little children?" asked Beth eagerly.

"I shall take the cream and the muffins," added Amy, heroically giving up the articles she liked most.

Meg was already covering the buckwheats, and piling the bread into one big plate.

"I thought you'd do it," said Mrs. March, smiling as if satisfied. "You shall all go and help me, and when we come back we will have bread and milk for breakfast, and make it up at dinnertime."

They were soon ready, and the procession set out. Fortunately it was early, and they went through back streets, so few people saw them, and no one laughed at the queer party.

A poor, bare, miserable room it was, with broken windows, no fire, ragged bedclothes, a sick mother, wailing baby, and a group of pale, hungry children cuddled under one old quilt, trying to keep warm.

How the big eyes stared and the blue lips smiled as the girls went in!

"Ach, mein Gott! it is good angels come to us!" said the poor woman, crying for joy.

"Funny angels in hoods and mittens," said Jo, and set them laughing.

In a few minutes it really did seem as if kind spirits had been at work there. Hannah, who had carried wood, made a fire, and stopped up the broken panes with old hats and her own cloak. Mrs. March gave the mother tea and gruel, and comforted her with promises of help, while she dressed the little baby as tenderly as if it had been her own. The girls, meantime, spread the table, set the children round the fire, and fed them like so many hungry birds — laughing, talking, and trying to understand the funny broken English.

"Das ist gut!" "Die Engel-kinder!" cried the poor things, as they ate, and warmed their purple hands at the comfortable blaze.

The girls had never been called angel children before, and thought it very agreeable, especially Jo, who had been considered a "Sancho" ever since she was born. That was a very happy breakfast, though they didn't get any of it; and when they went away, leaving comfort behind, I think there were not in all the city four merrier people than the hungry little girls who gave away their breakfasts and contented themselves with bread and milk on Christmas morning.

"That's loving our neighbor better than ourselves, and I like it," said Meg, as they set out their presents, while their mother was upstairs collecting clothes for the poor Hummels.

Not a very splendid show, but there was a great deal of love done up in the few little bundles; and the tall vase of red roses, white chrysanthemums, and trailing vines, which stood in the middle, gave quite an elegant air to the table.

"She's coming! Strike up, Beth! Open the door, Amy! Three cheers for Marmee!" cried Jo, prancing about, while Meg went to conduct mother to the seat of honor.

Beth played her gayest march, Amy threw open the door, and Meg enacted escort with great dignity. Mrs. March was both surprised and touched; and smiled with her eyes full as she examined her presents, and read the little notes which accompanied them. The slippers went on at once, a new handkerchief was slipped into her pocket, well scented with Amy's cologne, the rose was fastened in her bosom, and the the nice gloves were pronounced a "perfect fit."

There was a great deal of laughing and kissing and explaining, in the simple, loving fashion which makes these home festivals so pleasant at the time, so sweet to remember long afterward, and then all fell to work.

No Crib for a Bed

A manger is commonly recognized as a trough or open box used to hold feed for horses or cattle. At Christmas, however, it takes on a more sacred meaning, since a manger served as the first bed for our Lord Jesus Christ.

St. Francis of Assisi is credited with popularizing the use of a manger as part of Christmas celebrations. He wanted people to focus on Christmas' humble beginnings. "I desire to represent the birth of that Child in Bethlehem," he said, "in such a way that with our bodily eyes we may see all that He suffered for lack of the necessities for a newborn babe, and how He lay in the manger between the ox and the ass."

It was during a Christmas Eve mass in Greccio that St. Francis arranged his famous "crâche," or manger scene. This first crâche served as a model that is still widely used. The custom which he began in that Italian village soon spread to France, where it took on a life of its own. Manger scenes eventually became a fixture in family homes, and French craftsmen are credited with creating the unbaked clay figures known as "santons," or, "little saints." These are the figures you would expect to find at the original Christmas: the Holy Family, shepherds and Magi, ox and ass, and even, on occasion, other people who might have paid a visit to the newborn Babe.

Live performances of the manger scene began in twelfth-century France, spread throughout Europe and eventually the New World, and became more and more elaborate in scope as time went on. The household manger scenes also reached lofty heights; a crèche created in the sixteenth century for the first Grand Duke of Tuscany's son featured a mechanical crib with heavens that opened, and angels that flew above the scene and gradually came to earth.

At the Christmas markets of Europe today, it's common to find santons elaborate enough to relieve one of a substantial amount of money. (Not exactly what St. Francis had in mind!) But in most homes, you are likely to find well-worn, well-loved, slightly-the-worse-for-wear manger scenes that still remind us of how Christmas began and how simple its message remains to those who are able to "become as little children" and embrace the gentle Jesus.

— Essay by Debbie Titus George

WILLIAM DEAN HOWELLS
Christmas Every Day

The little girl came into her papa's study, as she always did Saturday morning before breakfast, and asked for a story. He tried to beg off that morning, for he was very busy, but she would not let him. So he began:

"Well, once there was a little pig —"

She stopped him at the word. She said she had heard little pig-stories till she was perfectly sick of them.

"Well, what kind of story *shall* I tell, then?"

"About Christmas. It's getting to be the season."

"Well!" Her papa roused himself. "Then I'll tell you about the little girl that wanted it Christmas every day in the year. How would you like that?"

"First-rate!" said the little girl, and she nestled into comfortable shape in his lap, ready for listening.

"Very well, then, this little pig — Oh, what are you pounding me for?"

"Because you said little pig instead of little girl."

"I should like to know what's the difference between a little pig and a little girl who wanted it Christmas every day!"

"Papa!" said the little girl warningly. At this her papa began to tell the story.

Once there was a little girl who liked Christmas so much that she wanted it to be Christmas every day in the year, and as soon as Thanksgiving was over she began to send postcards to the old Christmas Fairy to ask if she mightn't have it. But the old Fairy never answered, and after a while the little girl found out that the Fairy wouldn't notice anything but real letters sealed outside with a monogram — or your initial, anyway. So, then, she began to send letters, and just the day before Christmas, she got a letter from the Fairy, saying she might have it Christmas every day for a year, and then they would see about having it longer.

The little girl was excited already, preparing for the old-fashioned, once-a-year Christmas that was coming the next day. So she resolved to keep the Fairy's promise to herself and surprise everybody with it as it kept coming true, but then it slipped out of her mind altogether.

She had a splendid Christmas. She went to bed early, so as to let Santa Claus fill the stockings, and in the morning she was up the first of anybody and found hers all lumpy with packages of candy, and oranges and grapes, and rubber balls, and all kinds of small presents. Then she waited until the rest of the family was up, and she burst into the library to look at the large presents laid out on the library table — books, and boxes of stationery, and dolls, and little stoves, and dozens of handkerchiefs, and inkstands, and skates, and photograph frames, and boxes of watercolors, and dolls' houses — and the big Christmas tree, lighted and standing in the middle.

She had a splendid Christmas all day. She ate so much candy that she did not want any breakfast; and the whole forenoon the presents kept pouring in that had not been delivered the night before; and she went round giving the presents she had got for other people, and came home and ate turkey and cranberry for dinner, and plum pudding and nuts and raisins and oranges, and then went out and coasted, and came in with a stomachache, crying; and her papa said he would see if his house was turned into that sort of fool's paradise another year; and they had a light supper, and pretty early everybody went to bed cross.

The little girl slept very heavily and very late, but she was wakened at last by the other children dancing around her bed with their stockings full of presents in their hands. "Christmas! Christmas! Christmas!" they all shouted.

"Nonsense! It was Christmas yesterday," said the little girl, rubbing her eyes sleepily.

Her brothers and sisters just laughed. "We don't know about that. It's Christmas today, anyway. You come into the library and see."

Then all at once it flashed on the little girl that the Fairy was keeping her promise, and her year of Christmases was beginning. She was dreadfully sleepy, but she sprang up and darted into the library. There it was again! Books, and boxes of stationery, and dolls, and so on.

There was the Christmas tree blazing away, and the family picking out their presents, and her father looking perfectly puzzled, and her mother ready to cry. "I'm sure I don't see how I'm to dispose of all these things," said her mother, and her father said it seemed to him they had had something just like it the day before, but he supposed he must have dreamed it. This struck the little girl as the best kind of a joke, and so she ate so much candy she didn't want any breakfast, and went round carrying presents, and had turkey and cranberry for dinner, and then went out and coasted, and came in with a stomachache, crying.

Now, the next day, it was the same thing over again, but everybody getting crosser; and at the end of a week's time so many people had lost their tempers that you could pick up lost tempers anywhere; they perfectly strewed the ground. Even when people tried to recover their tempers they usually got somebody else's, and it made the most dreadful mix.

The little girl began to get frightened, keeping the secret all to herself; she wanted to tell her mother, but she didn't dare to; and she was ashamed to ask the Fairy to take back her gift, it seemed ungrateful and ill-bred. So it went on and on, and it was Christmas on St. Valentine's Day and Washington's birthday, just the same as any day, and it didn't skip even the First of April, though everything was counterfeit that day, and that was some little relief.

After a while turkeys got to be awfully scarce, selling for about a thousand dollars apiece. They got to passing off almost anything for turkeys — even half-grown hummingbirds. And cranberries — well, they asked a diamond apiece for cranberries. All the woods and orchards were cut down for Christmas trees. After a while they had to make Christmas trees out of rags. But there were plenty of rags, because people got so poor, buying presents for one another, that they couldn't get any new clothes, and they just wore their old ones to tatters. They got so poor that everybody had to go to the poorhouse, except the confectioners, and the storekeepers, and the booksellers; and they all got so rich and proud that they would hardly wait upon a person when he came to buy. It was perfectly shameful!

After it had gone on about three or four months, the little girl, whenever she came into the room in the morning and saw those great ugly, lumpy stockings dangling at the fireplace, and the disgusting presents around everywhere, used to sit down and burst out crying. In six months she was perfectly exhausted; she couldn't even cry anymore.

And how it was on the Fourth of July! On the Fourth of July, the first boy in the United States woke up and found out that his firecrackers and toy pistol and two-dollar collection of fireworks were nothing but sugar and candy painted up to look like fireworks. Before ten o'clock every boy in the United States discovered that his July Fourth things had turned into Christmas things and was so mad. The Fourth of July orations all turned into Christmas carols, and when anybody tried to read the Declaration of Independence, instead of saying, "When in the course of human events it becomes necessary," he was sure to sing, "God rest you merry gentlemen." It was perfectly awful.

About the beginning of October the little girl took to sitting down on dolls wherever she found them — she hated the sight of them so; and by Thanksgiving she just slammed her presents across the room. By that time people didn't carry presents around nicely anymore. They flung them over the fence or through the window, and, instead of taking great pains to write "For dear Papa," or "Mama," or "Brother," or "Sister," they used to write, "Take it, you horrid old thing!" and then go and bang it against the front door.

Nearly everybody had built barns to hold their presents, but pretty soon the barns overflowed, and then they used to let them lie out in the rain, or anywhere. Sometimes the police used to come and tell them to shovel their presents off the sidewalk or they would arrest them.

Before Thanksgiving came it had leaked out who had caused all these Christmases. The little girl had suffered so much that she had talked about it in her sleep, and after that hardly anybody would play with her, because if it had not been for her greediness it wouldn't have happened. And now, when it came Thanksgiving, and she wanted them to go to church, and have turkey, and show their gratitude, they said that all the turkeys had been eaten for her old Christmas dinners, and if she would stop the Christmases, they would see about the gratitude. And the very next day the little girl began sending letters to the Christmas Fairy, and then telegrams, to stop it. But it didn't do any good; and then she got to calling at the Fairy's house, but the girl that came to the door always said, "Not at home," or "Engaged," or something like that; and so it went on till it came to the old once-a-year Christmas Eve. The little girl fell asleep, and when she woke up in the morning —

"She found it was all nothing but a dream," suggested the little girl.

"No, indeed!" said her papa. "It was all every bit true!"

"What did she find out, then?"

"Why, that it wasn't Christmas at last, and wasn't ever going to be, anymore. Now it's time for breakfast."

The little girl held her papa fast around the neck.

"You shan't go if you're going to leave it so!"

"How do you want it left?"

"Christmas once a year."

"All right," said her papa; and he went on again.

Well, with no Christmas ever again, there was the greatest rejoicing all over the country. People met together everywhere and kissed and cried for joy. Carts went around and gathered up all the candy and raisins and nuts, and dumped them into the river; and it made the fish perfectly sick. And the whole United States, as far out as Alaska, was one blaze of bonfires, where the children were burning up their presents of all kinds. They had the greatest *time!*

The little girl went to thank the old Fairy because she had stopped its being Christmas, and she said she hoped the Fairy would keep her promise and see that Christmas never, never came again. Then the Fairy frowned, and said that now the little girl was behaving just as greedily as ever, and she'd better look out. This made the little girl think it all over carefully again, and she said she would be willing to have it Christmas about once in a thousand years; and then she said a hundred, and then she said ten, and at last she got down to one. Then the Fairy said that was the good old way that had pleased people ever since Christmas began, and she was agreed. Then the little girl said, "What're your shoes made of?" And the Fairy said, "Leather." And the little girl said, "Bargain's done forever," and skipped off, and hippity-hopped the whole way home, she was so glad.

"How will that do?" asked the papa.

"First-rate!" said the little girl; but she hated to have the story stop, and was rather sober. However, her mama put her head in at the door and asked her papa:

"Are you never coming to breakfast? What have you been telling that child?"

"Oh, just a tale with a moral."

The little girl caught him around the neck again.

"We know! Don't you tell *what*, papa! Don't you tell *what!*"

GEORGE MATTHEW ADAMS

The Christmas Heart

The Christmas heart is a beautiful heart for it is full of love and thoughtfulness for others.

And the Christmastime heart is a tribute to the most beautiful heart that ever beat.

It is also the time in which we are brought closest to our own inadequate abilities and helplessness of spirit. For we are so bathed with unselfishness that we feel our failures and lacks as never before in the entire year.

Perhaps it is well this way, so that we may resolve anew to live better and stronger lives for those who mean so much to us.

So let us cherish this Christmas heart and keep it a Christmas heart all through the year to come.

Let us put on all the lights in this heart so that it will be aglow to the world and let us push up the shades of the windows in this heart so that everyone who passes may be cheered and inspired.

Let us remember that the Christmas heart is a giving heart, a wide-open heart that thinks of others first.

The birth of the baby Jesus stands as the most significant event in all history, because it has meant the pouring into a sick world of the healing medicine of love which has transformed all manner of hearts for almost two thousand years and given beauty to human service it would never have had otherwise.

Underneath all the bulging bundles is this beating Christmas heart. Enwrapped about the tiniest gift is this same loveliness of thought and heart expression.

What a happy New Year for all if we would carry this same Christmas heart into every day during the coming year and make it a permanent thing in our lives. Let's do it!

CLEMENT C. MOORE

The Noel Candle

𝕴t was Christmas Eve in Rheims, nearly five hundred years ago. The great cathedral towered high above the city, its spires seemed to reach to the very skies, and the square in front of the church was thronged with people, celebrating the joyous Noel, the Christmas time. Children darted here and there through the crowd, shrieking with laughter. On one corner a group of well-dressed youths and maidens were dancing to the music of a lute and tambourine; in another a number of boys sang old carols. Others strolled about in groups of two and three, chatting and laughing, while the older and more serious went their way, candle in hand, toward the cathedral, where masses were being chanted in Latin. Though these churchgoers were more quiet, it was evident that they were happy, for their faces shone with contentment. It did not seem that there could be, in all the city of Rheims, one sad or lonely heart.

Yet there were four. Three of them dwelt in a squalid hovel by the riverside, a tiny shed or lean-to which stood beside a stable. Though its outward appearance was so dismal, once within the door, one might have been surprised to see how neat and trim it was kept. There was but one room which served at once as living room, dining room, bedroom and kitchen for three people. The rough stone floor was carefully swept and polished. In one corner lay a straw-filled mattress, but the covers drawn over it, though patched and darned in a dozen places, were spotlessly clean. A rude table, a broken chair, a stool and a clumsy bench completed the furniture of the room. In a far corner stood a small charcoal brazier, whose feeble fire served not only to cook the meals, but to warm the dwellers in the hut. Some cracked earthen kettles hung beside it.

The one touch of brightness and beauty in the little room was supplied by a tiny shrine, built on a shelf at the rear wall. A few field flowers in a bowl stood before it, and from the edge of the shelf hung a silken sash which once had held a knight's shield. It was of scarlet, heavily embroidered in gold, and bore a devise of a lion, surmounted by the lily of France.

Three people were in the room. A young woman was bending over a small spinning wheel, a boy of seven was setting the table with their few cracked dishes, and a girl a year or so older was leaning over a kettle on the brazier, stirring its contents from time to time. The lady, whose beauty seemed to shine in the poor room, despite her shabby clothing, was Madame la Comtesse Marie de Malincourt, and the boy and girl, her son and daughter, Louis and Jeanne.

As she worked the lady was thinking sadly of that Christmas Eve only a year before, when all had been so different. Then she had lived in a great castle, and on the eve of Noel, as she had done for a half dozen years before, she and her husband and the children had gone down to the castle gate to greet the crowd that had assembled. The old, the ailing, and the poor had gathered there, and that meant nearly all the village. Out among the crowd they had gone, followed by a dozen servants, laden down like beasts of burden and to each villager the lady had made gifts of warm clothing, of healing herbs, and of wholesome food. Even Louis and Jeanne, young as they were, had given from their store of toys and baubles to the children of the village.

Then the tide of war had swept over their happy valley; the castle had been attacked, defended, and lost, then sacked and pillaged by the victors. Lady Marie had even seen them lead her husband away a prisoner. She had fled with her children, down a secret passage out into the night and away to the village. She found it deserted, the villagers driven out before the sword.

During the months that had ensued the three had been wanderers along the highway. Bit by bit Lady Marie had given her jewels and trinkets, then those of the children, in exchange for food and lodging. Even her velvet robe, with its soft fur mantle, had gone to the wife of a rich burgher, and the pretty clothing of Louis and Jeanne had long since been replaced with coarse peasant garb. One thing alone remained of all their riches — the cover of her husband's shield, which little Louis had brought from the castle that dreadful night. "Father gave it to me to keep until he came back," he said, and through all the terrors of flight he had clung to it. It was very dear to them all. It seemed a bit of their old life, and a constant reminder of the dear lost father.

"Mother," said Jeanne suddenly, interrupting the current of her mother's sad thoughts, "it is Noel tonight."

"Yes, my child," Lady Marie answered with a sigh, "but there will be no toys, or sweets, or pretty things for thee or little Louis this Noel."

"We want them not," the children answered, almost in unison. "We have thee, dear mother, and we can keep the Noel in our hearts," added Jeanne.

Her mother looked up from the wheel and smiled at her. "Yes, though life is hard," she said, "still, we have each other, and though we are sad, perhaps there are other hearts in Rheims that grieve tonight. I wish I might give, as once I did, to the poor, but I have nothing to give. We have ourselves become the poor." She resumed her work, but there was silence in the room save for the whir of the wheel.

"Mother," Jeanne spoke again excitedly, "I know something we can give." As she talked she caught up the small tallow dip candle from the table and hurried with it to the one window of the hut.

"See," she went on, "I will put it here — on the sill — so — and perhaps someone who passes, someone like ourselves lonely and forlorn will be the happier for my little gift of light. There — see how it shines out on the snow," and she stood back to survey her work.

"You are a good child, Jeanne," said Lady Marie, then, sighing, she resumed her work, her silence, her sad thoughts.

Down in the great square, among all the lights and gayety, was another sad heart. It beat in the breast of a little lad of nine, a boy whose clothes were shabby and ragged, whose bare feet were thrust into clumsy wooden sabots, and with no covering on his head but his own fair hair. He was utterly alone, without money, without friends, cold, hungry, miserable. When it seemed he could bear this no longer he tried to tell his story to some of the smiling people he saw about him. Surely among so many he would find friends. But no one took any interest in him, other than to frown at him, or elbow him roughly out of the way, and one man shook him by the shoulder, and called him a beggar.

He left the square at last in utter discouragement, and began to tramp the streets, stopping now and then at splendid dwellings through whose windows streamed bright lights like a welcoming smile. But there was no welcome for the lonely child. Fat, well-dressed servants turned him away with angry words, and threatened him with their dogs.

It was dark in the streets of Rheims now, and the air was growing colder, but the child tramped on, trying desperately to find shelter before the night closed in. At last, far off down by the river, he saw a tiny gleam of light appear suddenly at a window and he hurried toward it. As he neared it, the boy saw that it was only a small tallow dip at the window of a hovel, the poorest and meanest hut in all Rheims, but the steady light of the tiny flame brought a sudden glow to his heart and he ran forward and knocked at the door.

It was opened in an instant by a little girl, and at once the other two in the room had risen to greet him. In another moment he found himself seated on a stool beside the charcoal brazier. The little girl was rubbing one of his cold hands in her two warm palms, while her brother was holding the other, and a beautiful woman, kneeling at his feet, drew off the wooden shoes, and chafed his icy feet. When he was thoroughly warmed, the little girl dished up into three bowls and a cracked cup the stew which had been simmering on the fire. There was only a little of it, a scant meal for themselves, but she passed the fullest bowl to the stranger and made room for him beside her on the bench.

After a word of blessing, they ate their stew, and never had the thin soup tasted so rich or so satisfying to the countess and her children. As they finished, a sudden glowing light filled the room, greater than the brightness of a thousand candles. There was a sound of angel voices, and the stranger child had grown so radiant they could scarcely bear to look at him.

"Thou, with thy little candle, has lighted the Christ-child on his way to heaven," said their unknown guest, his hand on the door latch. "This night shall thy dearest wish be granted thee," and in another instant he was gone.

The countess and her children fell on their knees and prayed, and there they still were, almost a quarter of an hour later, when a knight in armor gently pushed open the door and entered the hut.

"Marie! Jeanne! Louis!" he cried in a voice of love and longing. "Do you not know me after all these weary months of prison and battle, and then of search for thee?"

Immediately his family were clustered about him, and their kisses and embraces were his answer.

"But, father, how did you find us here," cried little Louis at last, when the first raptures of welcome were over.

"A ragged lad I met on the highway told me ye dwelt here," answered the knight.

"The Christ-child," said Lady Marie reverently, and told him the story.

And so, forever after, they and all their descendants, have burned a candle in the window on the eve of Noel, to light the lonely Christ-child on his way.

Baboushka

A RUSSIAN FOLK TALE

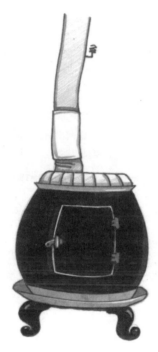

It was the night that Jesus was born in Bethlehem. In a faraway country an old woman named Baboushka sat in her snug little house by her warm fire. The wind was drifting the snow outside and howling down the chimney, but it only made Baboushka's fire burn more brightly.

"How glad I am to be indoors," said Baboushka, holding out her hands to the bright blaze.

Suddenly she heard a loud rap at her door. She opened it and there stood three splendidly dressed old men. Their beards were as white as the snow and so long they almost reached the ground. Their eyes shone kindly in the light of Baboushka's candle, and their arms were full of precious things — boxes of jewels and sweet-smelling oils and ointments.

"We have traveled far, Baboushka," they said, "and we have stopped to tell you of the babe born this night in Bethlehem. He has come to rule the world and teach us to be loving and true. We are bringing Him gifts. Come with us, Baboushka."

Baboushka looked at the swirling, drifting snow and then inside at her cozy room and the crackling fire. "It is too late for me to go with you, good sirs," she said. "The night is too cold." She shut the door and went inside and the old men journeyed to Bethlehem without her.

But as Baboushka sat rocking by her fire, she began to think about the baby Prince, for she loved babies.

"Tomorrow I will go to find Him," she said, "tomorrow, when it is light, and I will carry Him some toys."

In the morning Baboushka put on her long cloak and took her staff, and she filled her basket with the pretty things a baby would like, gold balls, and wooden toys and strings of silver cobwebs, and she set out to find the baby.

But Baboushka had forgotten to ask the three old men the way to Bethlehem, and they had traveled so far during the night that she could not catch up with them. Up and down the road she hurried, through the woods and fields and towns, telling everyone she met, "I am looking for the baby Prince. Where does He lie? I have some pretty toys for Him."

But no one could tell her the way. "Farther on, Baboushka, farther on," was their only reply. So she traveled on and on for years and years — but she never found the little Prince.

They say that Baboushka is traveling still, looking for Him. And every year, when Christmas Eve comes and all the children are lying fast asleep, Baboushka trudges softly through the snowy fields and towns, wrapped in her long cloak and carrying her basket on her arm. Gently she raps at every door.

"Is He here?" she asks. "Is the baby Prince here?" But the answer is always no, and sorrowfully she starts on her way again. Before she leaves, though, she lays a toy from her basket beside the pillow of each child. "For His sake," she says softly, and then hurries on through the years, forever in search of the baby Prince.

Based on The Nutcracker and The Mouse King by E.T.A. HOFFMANN
and The Nutcracker Ballet by PETER ILYICH TCHAIKOVSKY

Perhaps best known as a ballet, The Nutcracker is retold here in story form — a blending of the original short story and the ballet story line.

The Nutcracker

More than one hundred years ago on Christmas Eve, a twelve-year-old girl named Clara Stahlbaum and her younger brother Fritz were having a party at their house. Clara and Fritz peeked through a keyhole into the drawing room.

"What do you see?" Fritz asked.

"Nothing yet," Clara replied. "The grown-ups are just dancing and talking."

A moment later the door swung open and the parlor was flooded with light. "Merry Christmas, children!" Dr. Stahlbaum said. The time had come when they might join the party! The children raced past their father into the drawing room, with Fritz leading the way. Before them stood a Christmas tree at least ten feet tall! Beneath it were sugarplums, bonbons, toy soldiers, miniature swords and cannons, ceramic dolls, silk dresses, wooden horses, picture books, and dozens of other gifts. The children scurried about, discovering treasure after treasure. The grown-ups and children joined together in games and dances. Everything in the room seemed bright with candles and the fire crackled cheerfully.

Then the front door burst open and out of the winter night stepped a man dressed in black. He held a cape over his face and wore a tall hat. The click of his boots echoed off the marble floor and he entered the room. Slowly and dramatically, he drew aside his cape and the children were relieved to see the smiling face of Godpapa Drosselmeier, a master woodcarver in the village.

"Oh, Godpapa!" cried Clara, "you scared us!" Godpapa Drosselmeier gave her a big hug as he said, "My dear, I've brought you and the other children a surprise." He drew the sides of his cape together to make a great circle and three wooden figures stood on the floor in front of him: a prince, a princess, and a wicked-looking mouse wearing a crown. The figures began to move.

The mouse challenged the prince, they drew their swords, and a fight began. The children shouted encouragement. Finally, the prince defeated the mouse king, and then he kneeled, kissing the princess softly on her outstretched hand. Clara almost felt as if she could feel the kiss on her own hand.

When the wooden figures stopped moving, the guests clapped and cheered. Godpapa Drosselmeier took a bow, then turned to Clara and said, "And now, I have one more surprise. It's a special gift for a very special girl."

Godpapa drew his cape aside, and there stood another wooden figure wearing a handsome military uniform. Its face, though, was not handsome. Brightly painted, it had enormous eyes and a wide, gaping mouth. Still, something about the face filled Clara with tenderness. She picked up the figure and cradled it in her arms. Her eyes shone as she said, "Isn't this lovely?"

"Look closely at the wooden head," Godpapa said.

"His face is very sad," Clara thought, "but I like it."

"What is it?" the other children asked.

"It's a nutcracker," Godpapa answered. Then he took a walnut from his pocket and placed it in the little man's mouth. He closed the mouth and broke the nut.

"Let me do that!" said Fritz. He grabbed the nutcracker and tried to pull it away from his sister. There was a loud crack, and the wooden figure's head broke off.

"He's ruined!" Clara cried, holding her precious gift close and weeping bitterly.

"Now, now, my dear," said Godpapa Drosselmeier, taking the nutcracker from her. He put the wooden figure back together, and the nutcracker was as good as new. And from that moment Clara carried the little nutcracker doll with her everywhere, refusing to let anyone else hold it.

Meanwhile Fritz continued to drill his new toy soldiers with cries of "Bang, bang."

"My soldiers are brave and handsome," he said to Clara, "better than your ugly little doll."

"Take no notice of him," Clara whispered to the nutcracker. "He doesn't mean to be unkind." But the noise in the hot, crowded room made Fritz very excited and he marched up to Clara, snatched the little nutcracker and held it above his head. "Catch it if you can!" he yelled, dancing up and down. Clara tried to grab his arm but naughty Fritz hurled the little wooden doll across the room where it landed near the Christmas tree.

Just then, Clara's mother came to her and said, "It's supper time, Clara. Come and help me." Poor Clara had to leave her new toy where it had fallen.

Much later, the party was over and the children's friends went home, calling "Merry Christmas" to each other as they made their way through the snow to their carriages. Clara and Fritz went to bed and it was not long before everyone in the house was asleep — except for Clara. She could not stop thinking about the nutcracker. Finally, she slipped out of her bed, crept downstairs, and opened the drawing-room door. The drawing room was dark, but Clara had no trouble picking out the brightly painted face of the nutcracker beneath the Christmas tree. She went over to her new friend, lay down beside him, and fell into a deep sleep.

Suddenly, there was a noise in the room. Clara awoke and peered into the darkness. Slinking toward her was a mouse as big as a man. He was joined by ten others! They began running about, fighting and biting, and chewing all the presents under the Christmas tree! Then they began to circle around her, drawing closer and closer. When they were near enough to touch her, the clock chimed the first stroke of midnight.

Clara felt the nutcracker next to her beginning to move. Yawning and stretching, he rose to his feet and as the clock continued to strike, he began to grow. By the time the twelfth chime had died, he was a real-life soldier, standing six feet tall!

Clara watched as Nutcracker put one arm around her and, calling to the toy soldiers, the Nutcracker led them into a charge and the mice backed away. Then there was a puff of smoke and out stepped another mouse. Bigger and uglier than the others, he was the evil Mouse King, waving a sword of shining steel. Encouraged by the arrival of their leader, the other mice edged forward once again. The wooden swords of the toy soldiers were powerless against the steel blade of the Mouse King, and the Nutcracker had no sword at all. In a flash, Clara tore off her slipper and threw it across the room as hard as she could. It hit the Mouse King and he dropped his sword. The Nutcracker seized it, and with one stroke he cut off the King's head. At this, the other mice stopped fighting and scurried away to their holds.

Clara turned, and to her great surprise, the ugly little Nutcracker had been transformed into a handsome prince dressed in silver and white. He smiled down at her. "You've saved my life and broken a wicked spell, little Clara," he said. "Now I am free to go back to my country at last."

Then the prince sat Clara down under the Christmas tree and told her of his adventures.

Once upon a time, his story began, a queen quarreled with all the mice in her palace and banished them from her kingdom. As he slunk out of the hall, a wicked old wizard rat turned to the queen and squeaked, "You'll be sorry for this — and so will your daughter." The queen ran to her baby's crib, but too late. The baby's tiny cheeks were thin and hairy and whiskers grew under her pointed nose. She had been turned into a rat!

The grief-stricken queen called all the wisest men in her kingdom together, and they studied their magic books looking for a formula to break the wizard mouse's spell. They finally concluded that a Krakatuk tree must be found, one of its nuts must be picked, and then someone strong enough must be found to crack open the nut and give the kernel to the rat princess. As soon as she ate it, the spell would be broken. And so the wise men searched the kingdom, as did all the queen's subjects. At long last they found a Krakatuk tree nut and a young prince to open it. With a loud crack he split the shell and gave the kernel to the rat princess. She ate it, and instantly became a beautiful young girl again.

"Oh, thank you, thank you," cried the queen. But even as she spoke the prince began to grow smaller and smaller until he turned into a little wooden nutcracker. The wizard mouse squeaked with delight, "You may have your princess back, but you've lost the prince, and one day King Mouse will cut off his head!"

The prince explained to Clara, "And so I became an ugly little nutcracker. One day your godfather found me. He was sure you wouldn't mind my ugly face, and he was right. Thank you for saving my life. I must return to my country now. Would you like to come with me to the Kingdom of Sweets and visit my Sugar Palace?"

Clara was too excited to speak. She nodded yes, her eyes shining. And instantly, the Christmas tree before her began to grow taller and taller until its lights glittered like stars. The walls of the drawing room disappeared and Clara and the prince began to float through the shimmering moonlight in a walnut-shell boat. All around them, snowflake fairies danced to sweet music as they gently guided the boat to the shore of Candyland.

In Candyland, the prince and Clara stepped out of their boat and walked up an avenue laden with toffee apples, glittering sugarplums, and chocolate nuts. They passed cottages made of chocolate bars, with barley-sugar windows. The breeze smelled of honey and strawberry jam.

"It's so delicious!" Clara whispered, her eyes trying to take in all the strange sights. The nutcracker prince laughed as he said, "Just wait until you see my palace!" He pointed toward a mass of glittering towers that were barely visible through the trees.

Then, a beautiful Sugarplum Fairy came toward the Prince and Clara. "My snowflake fairies have told me what you did," she said, "and I want to thank you for saving our prince." She led Clara to a magnificent throne in the palace and said, "Tonight you are Queen Clara!"

With that, the celebration began! Sugar sticks twirled, chocolate drop cymbals clashed, a Chinese teapot and a set of Arabian coffee cups waltzed together, and a troupe of Cossacks leaped across the floor. Spun-sugar roses curtsied gracefully as the Prince invited the Sugarplum Fairy to dance. How the people cheered and clapped!

"Welcome to our prince," they shouted. "Hurrah for Clara! Hurrah for the Nutcracker! Hurrah! Hurrah!"

Clara blinked. Her eyes were dazzled by all the beauty before her.

Suddenly she heard a different voice. "Hurrah! It's Christmas Day!" The voice was that of her brother Fritz, shouting to her as she struggled to open her eyes. The dancers, the Sugarplum Fairy, and the Prince were gone, as was the Sugar Palace.

"It must have been a dream," Clara thought sadly.

Even so, years later . . . on her wedding day . . . Clara was reminded of the sugary towers as she gazed at her wedding cake, and as she looked closely, she was sure she glimpsed a
tiny sugarplum fairy dancing.

Hans Christian Andersen

The Fir Tree

Out in the woods stood a nice little Fir tree. The place he had was a very good one; the sun shone on him; as to fresh air, there was enough of that, and round him grew many large-sized comrades, pines as well as firs. But the little Fir wanted so very much to be a grown-up tree.

He did not think of the warm sun and of the fresh air; he did not care for the little cottage children that ran about and prattled when they were in the woods looking for wild strawberries. The children often came with a whole pitcherful of berries, or a long row of them threaded on a straw, and sat down near the young Tree and said, "Oh, how pretty he is! What a nice little Fir!" But this was what the Tree could not bear to hear.

At the end of the year he had shot up a good deal, and after another year he was another long bit taller; for with fir trees one can always tell by the shoots how many years old they are.

"Oh, were I but such a high tree as the others are!" sighed he. "Then I should be able to spread out my branches and with the tops look into the wide world! Then would the birds build nests among branches; and when there was a breeze I could bend with as much stateliness as the others!"

Neither the sunbeams, nor the birds, nor the red clouds which morning and evening sailed above him gave the little Tree any pleasure.

In winter, when the snow lay glittering on the ground, a hare would often come leaping along and jump right over the little Tree. Oh, that made him so angry! But two winters were past, and in the third the Tree was so large that the hare was obligated to go around it. "To grow and grow, to get older and be tall," thought the Tree — "that, after all, is the most delightful thing in the world!"

In autumn the woodcutters always came and felled some of the largest trees. This happened every year; and the young Fir tree, that had now grown to a very comely size, trembled at the sight; for the magnificent great trees fell to the earth with noise and cracking, the branches were lopped off, and the trees looked long and bare; they were hardly to be recognized; and then they were laid in carts, and the horses dragged them out of the woods.

Where did they go to? What became of them?

In spring, when the Swallows and the Storks came, the Tree asked them, "Don't you know where they have been taken? Have you not met them anywhere?"

The Swallows did not know anything about it; but the Stork looked musing, nodded his head, and said, "Yes, I think I know. I met many ships as I was flying hither from Egypt; on the ships were magnificent masts, and I venture to assert that it was they that smelt so of fir. I may congratulate you, for they lifted themselves on high most majestically!"

"Oh, were I but old enough to fly across the sea! But how does the sea look in reality? What is it like?"

"That would take a long time to explain," said the Stork; and with these words off he went.

"Rejoice in thy growth!" said the Sunbeams; "rejoice in the vigorous growth and in the fresh life that moveth within thee!"

And the Wind kissed the Tree, and the Dew wept tears over him, but the Fir understood it not.

When Christmas came, quite young trees were cut down, trees which often were not even as large or of the same age as this Fir tree who could never rest but always wanted to be off. These young trees, and they were always the finest-looking, retained their branches; they were laid on carts, and the horses drew them out of the woods.

"Where are they going to?" asked the Fir. "They are not taller than I; there was one indeed that was considerably shorter — and why do they retain all their branches? Whither are they taken?"

"We know! We know!" chirped the Sparrows. "We have peeped in at the windows in the town below! We know whither they are taken! The greatest splendor and the greatest magnificence one can imagine await them. We peeped through the windows and saw them planted in the middle of the warm room, and ornamented with the most splendid things — with gilded apples, with gingerbread, with toys, and many hundred lights!"

"And then?" asked the Fir tree, trembling in every bough. "And then? What happens then?"

"We did not see anything more; it was incomparably beautiful."

"I would fain know if I am destined for so glorious a career," cried the Tree, rejoicing. "That is still better than to cross the sea! What a longing do I suffer! Were Christmas but come! I am now tall, and my branches spread like the others that were carried off last year! Oh, were I but already on the cart! Were I in the warm room with all the splendor and magnificence! Yes; then something better, something still grander, will surely follow, or wherefore should they thus ornament me? Something better, something still grander, must follow — but what? Oh, how I long, how I suffer! I do not know myself what is the matter with me!"

"Rejoice in our presence!" said the Air and the Sunlight; "rejoice in thy own fresh youth!"

But the Tree did not rejoice at all; he grew and grew, and was green both winter and summer. People that saw him said, "What a fine tree!" and toward Christmas he was one of the first that was cut down. The ax struck deep into the very pith; the tree fell to the earth with a sigh; he felt a pang — it was like a swoon; he could not think of happiness, for he was sorrowful at being separated from his home, from the place where he had sprung up. He well knew that he should never see his dear old comrades, the little bushes and flowers around him, anymore, perhaps not even the birds! The departure was not at all agreeable.

The Tree only came to himself when he was unloaded in a courtyard with the other trees, and heard a man say, "That one is splendid; we don't want the others." Then two servants came in rich livery and carried the Fir tree into a large and splendid drawing room. Portraits were hanging on the walls, and near the white porcelain stove stood two large Chinese vases with lions on the covers. There, too, were large easy chairs, silken sofas, large tables full of picture books and full of toys worth hundreds and hundreds of crowns — at least the children said so. And the Fir tree was stuck upright in a cask that was filled with sand; but no one could see that it was a cask, for green cloth was hung all around it, and it stood on a large, gaily colored carpet. Oh, how the tree quivered! What was to happen? The servants as well as the young ladies decorated it. On one branch there hung little nets cut out of colored paper, and each net was filled with sugarplums; and among the other boughs gilded apples and walnuts were suspended, looking as though they had grown there, and little blue and white tapers were placed among the leaves. Dolls that looked for all the world like men — the Tree had never beheld such before — were seen among the foliage, and at the very top a large star of gold tinsel was fixed. It was really splendid — beyond description splendid.

"This evening!" said they all; "how it will shine this evening!"

"Oh," thought the Tree, "if the evening were but come! If the tapers were but lighted! And then I wonder what will happen! Perhaps the other trees from the forest will come to look at me! Perhaps the sparrows will beat against the windowpanes! I wonder if I shall take root here and winter and summer stand covered with ornaments."

He knew very much about the matter! But he was so impatient that for sheer longing he got a pain in his back, and this with trees is the same thing as a headache with us.

The candles were now lighted. What brightness! What splendor! The Tree trembled so in every bough that one of the tapers set fire to the foliage. It blazed up splendidly.

"Help! help!" cried the young ladies, and they quickly put out the fire.

Now the Tree did not even dare tremble. What a state he was in! He was so uneasy lest he should lose something of his splendor that he was quite bewildered amid the glare and brightness, when suddenly both folding doors opened and a troop of children rushed in as if they would upset the Tree. The older persons followed quietly; the little ones stood quite still. But it was only for a moment; then they shouted so that the whole place re-echoed with their rejoicing; they danced round the Tree, and one present after the other was pulled off.

"What are they about?" thought the Tree. "What is to happen now?" And the lights burned down to the very branches, and as they burned down they were put out one after the other, and then the children had permission to plunder the Tree. So they fell upon it with such violence that all its branches cracked; if it had not been fixed firmly in the cask it would certainly have tumbled down.

The children danced about with their beautiful playthings; no one looked at the Tree except the old nurse, who peeped between the branches; but it was only to see if there was a fig or an apple left that had been forgotten.

"A story! A story!" cried the children, drawing a little fat man toward the Tree. He seated himself under it and said, "Now we are in the shade, and the Tree can listen too. But I shall tell only one story. Now which will you have: that about Ivedy-Avedy, or about Klumpy-Dumpy who tumbled downstairs, and yet after all came to the throne and married the princess?"

"Ivedy-Avedy," cried some; "Klumpy-Dumpy," cried the others. There was such a bawling and screaming. The Fir tree alone was silent, and he thought to himself, "Am I not to bawl with the rest — am I to do nothing whatever?" for he was one of the company and had done what he had to do.

And the man told about Klumpy-Dumpy that tumbled down, who notwithstanding came to the throne and at last married the princess. And the children clapped their hands and cried out, "Oh, go on! Do go on!" They wanted to hear about Ivedy-Avedy, too, but the little man only told them about Klumpy-Dumpy. The Fir tree stood quite still and absorbed in thought; the birds in the woods had never related the like of this.

"Klumpy-Dumpy fell downstairs, and yet he married the princess! Yes, yes! That's the way of the world!" thought the Fir tree, and believed it all, because the man who told the story was so good-looking. "Well, well! Who knows, perhaps I may fall downstairs, too, and get a princess as a wife!" And he looked forward with joy to the morrow, when he hoped to be decked out again with lights, playthings, fruits, and tinsel.

"I won't tremble tomorrow!" thought the Fir tree. "I will enjoy to the full all my splendor! Tomorrow I shall hear again the story of Klumpy-Dumpy, and perhaps that of Ivedy-Avedy, too." And the whole night the Tree stood still and in deep thought.

In the morning the servant and the housemaid came in.

"Now, then, the splendor will begin again," thought the Fir, but they dragged him out of the room, and up the stairs into the loft; and here in a dark corner, where no daylight could enter, they left him. "What's the meaning of this?" thought the Tree. "What am I to do here? What shall I hear now, I wonder?" And he leaned against the wall, lost in reverie. Time enough had he, too, for his reflections, for days and nights passed on, and nobody came up; and when at last somebody did come it was only to put some great trunks in a corner out of the way. There stood the Tree, quite hidden; it seemed as if he had been entirely forgotten.

"'Tis now winter out-of-doors!" thought the Tree. "The earth is hard and covered with snow; men cannot plant me now, and therefore I have been put up here under shelter till the springtime comes! How thoughtful that is! How kind man is, after all! If it only were not too dark here and so terribly lonely! Not even a hare. And out in the woods it was so pleasant when the snow was on the ground, and the hare leaped by; yes, even when he jumped over me; but I did not like it then. It is really terribly lonely here!"

"Squeak! Squeak!" said a little Mouse, at the same moment peeping out of his hole. And then another little one came.

They snuffed about the Fir tree and rustled among the branches.

"It is dreadfully cold," said the Mouse. "But for that it would be delightful here, old Fir, wouldn't it?"

"I am by no means old," said the Fir tree. "There's many a one considerably older than I am."

"Where do you come from," asked the Mice, "and what can you do?" They were so extremely curious. "Tell us about the most beautiful spot on the earth. Have you never been there? Were you never in the larder where cheeses lie on the shelves and hams hang from above, where one dances about on tallow candles; that place where one enters lean and comes out again fat and portly?"

"I know no such place," said the Tree. "But I know the woods, where the sun shines, and where the little birds sing." And then he told all about his youth; and the little Mice had never heard the like before; and they listened and said, "Well, to be sure! How much you have seen! How happy you must have been!"

"I!" said the Fir tree, thinking over what he had himself related. "Yes, in reality those were happy times." And then he told about Christmas Eve, when he was decked out with cakes and candles.

"Oh," said the little Mice, "how fortunate you have been, old Fir tree!"

"I am by no means old," said he. "I came from the woods this winter; I am in my prime, and am only rather short for my age."

"What delightful stories you know!" said the Mice; and the next night they came with four other little Mice, who were to hear what the Tree recounted; and the more he related the more plainly he remembered all himself; and it appeared as if those times had really been happy times. "But they may still come — they may still come. Klumpy-Dumpy fell downstairs, and yet he got a princess!" And he thought at the moment of a nice little Birch tree growing out in the wood; to the Fir that would be a real charming princess.

"Who is Klumpy-Dumpy?" asked the Mice. So then the Fir tree told the whole fairy tale, for he could remember every single word of it; and the little Mice jumped for joy up to the very top of the Tree. The next night two more Mice came, and on Sunday two Rats, even; but they said the stories were not interesting, which vexed the little Mice; and they, too, now began to think them not so very amusing, either.

"Do you know only one story?" asked the Rats.

"Only that one," answered the Tree. "I heard it on my happiest evening; but I did not then know how happy I was."

"It is a very stupid story! Don't you know one about bacon and tallow candles? Can't you tell any larder stories?"

"No," said the Tree.

"Then good-by," said the Rats; and they went home.

At last the little Mice stayed away also; and the Tree sighed. "After all, it was very pleasant when the sleek little Mice sat around me and listened to what I told them. Now that, too, is over. But I will take good care to enjoy myself when I am brought out again."

But when was that to be? Why, one morning there came a quantity of people and set to work in the loft. The trunks were moved, the Tree was pulled out and thrown — rather hard, it is true — down on the floor, but a man drew him toward the stairs, where the daylight shone.

"Now a merry life will begin again," thought the Tree. He felt the fresh air, the first sunbeam — and now he was out in the courtyard. All passed so quickly, there was so much going on around him, that the Tree quite forgot to look to himself. The court adjoined a garden, and all was in flower; the roses hung so fresh and odorous over the balustrade, the lindens were in blossom, the Swallows flew by and said, "Quirre-vit! My husband is come!" but it was not the Fir tree that they meant.

"Now, then, I shall really enjoy life," said he, exultingly, and — spread out his branches; but alas! they were all withered and yellow. It was in a corner that he lay, among weeds and nettles. The golden star of tinsel was still on the top of the Tree, and glittered in the sunshine.

In the courtyard some of the merry children were playing who had danced at Christmas round the Fir tree and were so glad at the sight of him. One of the youngest ran and tore off the golden star.

"Only look what is still on the ugly old Christmas tree!" said he, trampling on the branches so that they all cracked beneath his feet.

And the tree beheld all the beauty of the flowers and the freshness in the garden; he beheld himself and wished he had remained in his dark corner in the loft; he thought of his first youth in the wood, of the merry Christmas Eve, and of the little Mice who had listened with so much pleasure to the story of Klumpy-Dumpy.

" 'Tis over! 'Tis past!" said the poor Tree. "Had I but rejoiced when I had reason to do so! But now 'tis past, 'tis past!"

And the gardener's boy chopped the Tree into small pieces; there was a heap lying there. The wood flamed up splendidly under the large brewing cauldron, and it sighed so deeply! Each sigh was like a shot.

The boys played about in the court, and the youngest wore the gold star on his breast which the Tree had had on the happiest evening of his life. However, that was over now — the Tree gone, the story at an end. All, all was over; every tale must end at last.

SELMA LAGERLÖF

The Holy Night

There was a man who went out in the dark night to borrow live coals to kindle a fire. He went from hut to hut and knocked. "Dear friends, help me!" said he. "My wife has just given birth to a child, and I must make a fire to warm her and the little one."

But it was way in the night, and all the people were asleep. No one replied.

The man walked and walked. At last he saw the gleam of a fire a long way off. Then he went in that direction, and saw that the fire was burning in the open. A lot of sheep were sleeping around the fire, and an old shepherd sat and watched over the flock.

When the man who wanted to borrow fire came up to the sheep, he saw that three big dogs lay asleep at the shepherd's feet. All three awoke when the man approached and opened their great jaws, as though they wanted to bark; but not a sound was heard. The man noticed that the hair on their backs stood up and that their sharp, white teeth glistened in the firelight. They dashed toward him.

He felt that one of them bit at his leg and one at his hand and that one clung to his throat. But their jaws and teeth wouldn't obey them, and the man didn't suffer the least harm.

Now the man wished to go farther, to get what he needed. But the sheep lay back to back and so close to one another that he couldn't pass them. Then the man stepped upon their backs and walked over them and up to the fire. And not one of the animals awoke or moved.

When the man had almost reached the fire, the shepherd looked up. He was a surly old man, who was unfriendly and harsh toward human beings. And when he saw the strange man coming, he seized the long, spiked staff, which he always held in his hand when he tended his flock, and threw it at him. The staff came right toward the man, but, before it reached him, it turned off to one side and whizzed past him, far out in the meadow.

Now the man came up to the shepherd and said to him: "Good man, help me, and lend me a little fire! My wife has just given birth to a child, and I must make a fire to warm her and the little one."

The shepherd would rather have said no, but when he pondered that the dogs couldn't hurt the man, and the sheep had not run from him, and that the staff had not wished to strike him, he was a little afraid, and dared not deny the man that which he asked.

"Take as much as you need!" he said to the man.

But then the fire was nearly burnt out. There were no logs or branches left, only a big heap of live coals; and the stranger had neither spade nor shovel wherein he could carry the red-hot coals.

When the shepherd saw this, he said again: "Take as much as you need!" And he was glad that the man wouldn't be able to take away any coals.

But the man stooped and picked coals from the ashes with his bare hands, and laid them in his mantle. And he didn't burn his hands when he touched them, nor did the coals scorch his mantle; but he carried them away as if they had been nuts or apples.

And when the shepherd, who was such a cruel and hard-hearted man, saw all this, he began to wonder to himself: What kind of a night is this, when the dogs do not bite, the sheep are not scared, the staff does not kill, or the fire scorch? He called the stranger back and said to him: "What kind of a night is this? And how does it happen that all things show you compassion?"

Then said the man: "I cannot tell you if you yourself do not see it." And he wished to go his way, that he might soon make a fire and warm his wife and child.

But the shepherd did not wish to lose sight of the man before he had found out what all this might portend. He got up and followed the man till they came to the place where he lived.

Then the shepherd saw that the man didn't have so much as a hut to dwell in, but that his wife and babe were lying in a mountain grotto, where there was nothing except the cold and naked stone walls.

But the shepherd thought that perhaps the poor innocent child might freeze to death there in the grotto; and, although he was a hard man, he was touched, and thought he would like to help it. And he loosened his knapsack from his shoulder, took from it a soft white sheepskin, gave it to the strange man, and said that he should let the child sleep on it.

But just as soon as he showed that he, too, could be merciful, his eyes were opened, and he saw what he had not been able to see before, and heard what he could not have heard before.

He saw that all around him stood a ring of little silver-winged angels, and each held a stringed instrument, and all sang in loud tones that tonight the Saviour was born Who should redeem the world from its sins.

Then he understood how all things were so happy this night that they didn't want to do anything wrong.

And it was not only around the shepherd that there were angels, but he saw them everywhere. They sat inside the grotto, they sat outside on the mountain, and they flew under the heavens. They came marching in great companies, and, as they passed, they paused and cast a glance at the child.

There were such jubilation and such gladness and songs and play! And all this he saw in the dark night, whereas before he could not have made out anything. He was so happy because his eyes had been opened that he fell upon his knees and thanked God.

What that shepherd saw, we might also see, for the angels fly down from heaven every Christmas Eve, if we could only see them.

You must remember this, for it is as true, as true as that I see you and you see me. It is not revealed by the light of lamps or candles, and it does not depend upon sun and moon; but that which is needful is that we have such eyes as can see God's glory.

VERA E. WALKER

What really happened to the Holy Family when they fled Bethlehem and sought sanctuary in Egypt? Perhaps they had experiences such as these.

Legends of the Flight Into Egypt

Long, long ago, on that dark and sorrowful night, when Herod had made up his mind to kill the Child born to be King, His father and mother stole out of Bethlehem and made their way towards the far-off land of Egypt for safety. The light of Joseph's lantern made strange shadows flicker along the narrow street as he led the little ass forward, and Mary drew her cloak closer round the Babe as if to shield Him from evil. Perhaps the watchman at the gate knew them, for he let them through without asking where they were going.

They went quickly, lest Herod's spies should be at work even now, yet not as if in fear. They went along the ridges of the stony hills first, and then climbed down into the plains and turned their faces towards the blue sea and the desert country that lies between Palestine and Egypt, choosing paths which travellers rarely followed. It was in these lonely places, full of dangers, that many strange and beautiful happenings took place.

It was not long before they found themselves hungry in the desert, for they had left Bethlehem in haste and taken little with them. Wondering what was to become of them, they came suddenly to a tall palm tree, where dates grew, but so high up that it was impossible to reach them; so they sat down to rest in the shade. As they gazed up into the green leaves, Mary heard the Babe cooing softly to Himself, and turning, she saw a cluster of dates fallen to the earth close by Him, just as if the tree herself had longed to help them and dropped her fruit to give them food. So they ate and were refreshed and went on.

Everywhere they went with the Babe all dumb or living creatures lent them their help. Sometimes, when they were tired and thirsty, a fresh spring would gush out close by, although it had seemed that no water was there when they looked last. Once, a mother goat came to them and gave them her milk. She seemed as if she had known them all her life. Once, as Mary lay down to rest on the harsh dry sand, she smelt a sweet scent all around and, putting out her hand, she touched a little starry golden flower that had sprung up to make a couch for herself and the Babe. Once, when she was washing His clothes, she found a little grey-green plant, sweet as a rose, growing all ready for her to spread them over it. So tree and flower helped them on their way.

They travelled by night mostly, for the day was too hot for walking, and as they went the wild creatures of the desert came out of their dens in search of food. The little grey jackals moved like swift shadows about them; the desert birds circled round their heads; lions roared in the distance. Yet all seemed friendly. The jackals would trot by their side without snarling; the lions walked with them as a bodyguard; the birds flew peacefully overhead. In the presence of the Babe of Bethlehem the creatures were at peace with one another and did no harm. And the Babe smiled on the wild things of the night, and in the daytime laughed at the bright insects and the lizards flashing over the sun-baked stones.

Near Egypt they came to a dark place leading through a woods, and as they went a band of robbers rushed out to meet them. They were fierce, rough men, who thought nothing of killing an old man for the sake of his ass or the few goods he carried with him. But, as the young chief came forward he saw the Babe smiling in His mother's arms, and he gave an order that checked his men, and spoke kindly to the travellers. Still looking at the Babe, he led them into his cave and begged them to rest there till morning. The robber's wife brought them cakes and honey and fruit, and they lay down peacefully to sleep. The next morning they found the cave full of fierce robbers, who had come in to look at them, but the Babe smiled at them and Mary and Joseph had no fear. Then the chief entered, and taking them outside, showed them a good road which would take them where they wished to go. "Farewell," he said to them as they rode away, "and in whatever place you are remember me who has lodged you this night."

So the travellers passed on, and came quickly to the land of Egypt, where they lived safely until news of Herod's death reached them.

S E T H P A R K E R

Silas Tucker Discovers Christmas

Silas Tucker who used ter live over ter Columbia Falls, weren't much of a feller fer thinking of others. He ran the little newspaper and he was so busy rushing here and there that he hardly had time to give folks change when they paid him their bills.

Silas didn't have much use fer Christmas, neither. He thought of it as a day when you had to hold up your work, and if he'd had his way he wouldn't even have knowed what day it was; but folks kept talking about it, so he couldn't help knowing it was Thursday.

Thursday morning he got up earlier than the rest of the family and kept grunting to himself about its being Christmas. But on the way down the street he seen Tom Harriman, and seeing Tom was a heavy advertiser in the paper, Silas says, "Merry Christmas," and he about fell over when Tom doubled up so hard with laughing he couldn't stand straight.

Silas went on, kind of tickled at himself for being so smart, and when he seen Sam Fletcher he yelled out "Merry Christmas," and Sam laughed and slapped him on the back and thought it was a great joke.

By the time Silas had got to the office, he'd yelled "Merry Christmas" to a dozen folks and they had all called him so clever he was feeling real good, and when he went in the office he yelled out to all what was there, "Merry Christmas to yer." They laughed and called out to him and had a great time, and when Silas got alone in his office he set down real tickled with himself. He could hear the folks outside calling "Merry Christmas" to each other and laughing, and it give him quite a kick.

He enjoyed it so much that about ten o'clock in the morning he went out in the main office and sez to them, "If you can get your day's work done by three o'clock you can all go home, seeing it's Christmas." They laughed and cheered him, and long before three o'clock come they had more than a day's work done so he let them go and they went off singing his praises and what a wonderful man he was.

Well, seeing no more to be done, Silas went out and bought a dress for his wife, Jane, and took it home and give it to her. She was so surprised she didn't know whether he'd gone crazy or feeble-minded, and then he sez to her, "I'm surprised you didn't get a Christmas tree today."

"Didn't get a Christmas tree for today?" she sez. "What are you talking about?"

"Ain't today Christmas?" he sez.

"Land of Betsy," says Jane, "Christmas ain't until next Thursday."

Well sir, Silas put back his head and laughed so hard he could hardly set in the chair. "And to think," sez he, "I got more work done today than I ever did and got more fun out of it, and it weren't Christmas after all."

If you go up to Columbia Falls some time and ask about Silas Tucker, they'll tell you he's the salt of the earth, but they'll also tell you that he's a mite queer. He's got a funny sense of humor, is the way they explain it. When business is poor or Silas gets to feeling blue, he'll pull off what he calls an independent Christmas. He yells "Merry Christmas" to everybody he sees, shuts down early, buys folks presents, and chuckles about it from morning to night.

And what's more, the last time I heard he hadn't even got the idee patented.

HENRY VAN DYKE

How many wise men came to worship the young child Jesus?
The Scriptures don't say, but what we do know is that
the wise men sought Jesus until they found Him.

The Other Wise Man

I.

𝕴n the days when Augustus Caesar was master of many kings and Herod reigned in Jerusalem, there lived in the city of Ecbatana, among the mountains of Persia, a certain man named Artaban. His house stood close to the outermost of the walls which encircled the royal treasury. From his roof he could look over the sevenfold battlements of black and white and crimson and blue and red and silver and gold, to the hill where the summer palace of the Parthian emperors glittered like a jewel in a crown.

Around the dwelling of Artaban spread a fair garden, a tangle of flowers and fruit trees, watered by a score of streams descending from the slopes of Mount Orontes, and made musical by innumerable birds. But all color was lost in the soft and odorous darkness of the late September night, and all sounds were hushed in the deep charm of its silence, save the splashing of the water, like a voice half sobbing and half laughing under the shadows. High above the trees a dim glow of light shone through the curtained arches of the upper chamber, where the master of the house was holding council with his friends.

He stood by the doorway to greet his guests — a tall, dark man of about forty years, with brilliant eyes set near together under his broad brow, and firm lines graven around his fine, thin lips; the brow of a dreamer and the mouth of a soldier, a man of sensitive feeling but inflexible will — one of those who, in whatever age they may live, are born for inward conflict and a life of quest.

His robe was of pure white wool, thrown over a tunic of silk; and a white, pointed cap, with long lapels at the sides, rested on his flowing black hair. It was the dress of the Magi.

"Welcome!" he said, in his low, pleasant voice, as one after another entered the room.

"You have come tonight," said he, looking around the circle, "at my call to renew your worship and rekindle your faith in the God of Purity. We worship not the fire, but Him of whom it is the chosen symbol, because it is the purest of all created things. It speaks to us of one who is Light and Truth.

"It was the Hebrew Daniel, the mighty searcher of dreams, the counselor of kings, the wise Belteshazzar, who was most honored and beloved of our great King Cyrus. A prophet of sure things and a reader of the thoughts of the Eternal, Daniel proved himself to our people. And these are the words that he wrote."

(Artaban read from [a scroll]:) " 'Know, therefore, and understand that from the going forth of the commandment to restore Jerusalem, unto the Anointed One, the Prince, the time shall be seven and threescore and two weeks.' "

"But my son," said Abgarus, doubtfully, "these numbers . . . who can interpret them, or who can find the key that shall unlock their meaning?"

Artaban answered: "It has been shown to me and to my three companions among the Magi — Caspar, Melchior and Balthasar. We have searched the ancient tablets of Chaldea and computed the time. It falls in this year. We saw a new star, which shone for one night and then vanished. If the star shines again, they will wait ten days for me at the temple, and then we will set out together for Jerusalem, to see and worship the promised one who shall be born King of Israel. I believe the sign will come. I have made ready for the journey. I have sold my possessions, and bought these three jewels — a sapphire, a ruby and a pearl — to carry them as tribute to the King. And I ask you to go with me on the pilgrimage, that we may have joy together in finding the Prince who is worthy to be served."

While he was speaking he thrust his hand into the inmost fold of his girdle and drew out three great gems — one blue as a fragment of the night sky, one redder than a ray of sunrise, and one as pure as the peak of a snow mountain at twilight — and laid them on the outspread scrolls before him.

But his friends looked on with strange and alien eyes. A veil of doubt and mistrust came over their faces, like a fog creeping up from the marshes to hide the hills. They glanced at each other with looks of wonder and pity, as those who have listened to incredible sayings, the story of a wild vision, or the proposal of an impossible enterprise.

At last Tigranes said: "Artaban, this is a vain dream. It comes from too much looking upon the stars and the cherishing of lofty thoughts. It would be wiser to spend the time in gathering money. No king will ever rise from the broken race of Israel, and no end will ever come to the eternal strife of light and darkness. He who looks for it is a chaser of shadows. Farewell."

So, one by one, they left the house of Artaban. But Abgarus, the oldest and the one who loved him the best, lingered after the others had gone, and said, gravely: "My son, it may be that the light of truth is in this sign that has appeared in the skies, and then it will surely lead to the Prince and the mighty brightness. Or it may be that it is only a shadow of the light, as Tigranes has said, and then he who follows it will have a long pilgrimage and a fruitless search. But it is better to follow even the shadow of the best than to remain content with the worst. And those who would see wonderful things must often be ready to travel alone. I am too old for this journey, but my heart shall be a companion of thy pilgrimage day and night, and I shall know the end of thy quest. Go in peace."

Then Abgarus went out of the azure chamber with its silver stars, and Artaban was left in solitude.

He gathered up the jewels and replaced them in his girdle. For a long time he stood and watched the flame that flickered and sank. Then he crossed the hall, lifted the heavy curtain, and passed out between the pillars of porphyry to the terrace on the roof.

Far over the eastern plain a white mist stretched like a lake. But where the distant peaks of Zagros serrated the western horizon the sky was clear. Jupiter and Saturn rolled together like drops of lambent flame about to blend in one.

As Artaban watched them, a steel-blue spark was born out of the darkness beneath, rounding itself with purple splendors to a crimson sphere, and spring upward through rays of saffron and orange into a point of white radiance. Tiny and infinitely remote, yet perfect in every part, it pulsated in the enormous vault as if the three jewels in the Magian's girdle had mingled and been transformed into a living heart of light.

He bowed his head. He covered his brow with his hands.

"It is the sign," he said. "The King is coming, and I will go to meet him."

II.

All night long, Vasda, the swiftest of Artaban's horses, had been waiting, saddled and bridled, in her stall, pawing the ground impatiently and shaking her bit as if she shared the eagerness of her master's purpose, though she knew not its meaning.

Before the birds had fully roused to their strong, high, joyful chant of morning song, before the white mist had begun to lift lazily from the plain, the Other Wise Man was in the saddle, riding swiftly along the highroad, which skirted the base of Mount Orontes, westward.

Artaban must indeed ride wisely and well if he would keep the appointed hour with the other Magi; for the route was a hundred and fifty parasangs, and fifteen was the utmost that he could travel in a day. But he knew Vasda's strength, and pushed forward without anxiety, making the fixed distance every day, though he must travel late into the night, and in the morning long before sunrise.

Artaban pressed onward until he arrived, at nightfall on the tenth day, beneath the shattered walls of populous Babylon.

Vasda was almost spent, and Artaban would gladly have turned into the city to find rest and refreshment for himself and for her. But he knew that it was three hours' journey yet, and he must reach the place by midnight if he would find his comrades waiting. So he did not halt, but rode steadily across the stubble fields.

A grove of date palms made an island of gloom in the pale yellow sea. As she passed into the shadow Vasda slackened her pace, and began to pick her way more carefully.

Near the farther end of the darkness an access of caution seemed to fall upon her. She scented some danger or difficulty; it was not in her heart to fly from it — only to be prepared for it, and to meet it wisely, as a good horse should do. The grove was close and silent as the tomb; not a leaf rustled, not a bird sang.

She felt her steps before her delicately, carrying her head low, and sighing now and then with apprehension. At last she gave a quick breath of anxiety and dismay, and stood stock-still, quivering in every muscle, before a dark object in the shadow of the last palm tree.

Artaban dismounted. The dim starlight revealed the form of a man lying across the road. His humble dress and the outline of his haggard face showed that he was probably one of the Hebrews who still dwelt in great numbers around the city. His pallid skin, dry and yellow as parchment, bore the mark of the deadly fever which ravaged the marshlands in autumn. The chill of death was in his lean hand, and, as Artaban released it, the arm fell back inertly upon the motionless breast.

He turned away with a thought of pity, leaving the body to that strange burial which the Magians deemed most fitting — the funeral of the desert, from which the kites and vultures rise on dark wings, and the beasts of prey slink furtively away. When they are gone there is only a heap of white bones on the sand.

But, as he turned, a long, faint, ghostly sigh came from the man's lips. The bony fingers gripped the hem of the Magian's robe and held him fast.

Artaban's heart leaped to his throat, not with fear, but with a dumb resentment at the importunity of this blind delay.

How could he stay here in the darkness to minister to a dying stranger? What claim had this unknown fragment of human life upon his compassion or his service? If he lingered but for an hour he could hardly reach Borsippa at the appointed time. His companions would think he had given up the journey. They would go without him. He would lose his quest.

But if he went on now, the man would surely die. If Artaban stayed, life might be restored. His spirit throbbed and fluttered with the urgency of the crisis. Should he risk the great reward of his faith for the sake of a single deed of charity? Should he turn aside, if only for a moment, from the following of the star, to give a cup of cold water to a poor, perishing Hebrew?

"God of truth and purity," he prayed, "direct me in the holy path, the way of wisdom which Thou only knowest."

Then he turned back to the sick man. Loosening the grasp of his hand, he carried him to a little mound at the foot of the palm tree.

He unbound the thick folds of the turban and opened the garment above the sunken breast. He brought water from one of the small canals nearby, and moistened the sufferer's brow and mouth. He mingled a draught of one of those simple but potent remedies which he carried always in his girdle — for the Magians were physicians too — and poured it slowly between the colorless lips. Hour after hour he labored as only a skillful healer of disease can do. At last the man's strength returned; he sat up and looked about him.

"Who art thou?" he said, in the rude dialect of the country, "and why hast thou sought me here to bring back my life?"

"I am Artaban the Magian, of the city of Ecbatana and I am going to Jerusalem in search of one who is to be born King of the Jews, a great Prince and Deliverer of all men. I dare not delay any longer upon my journey, for the caravan that has waited for me may depart without me. But see, here is all that I have left of bread and wine, and here is a potion of healing herbs. When thy strength is restored thou canst find the dwellings of the Hebrews among the houses of Babylon."

The Jew raised his trembling hand solemnly to heaven.

"Now may the God of Abraham and Isaac and Jacob bless and prosper the journey of the merciful, and bring him in peace to his desired haven. Stay! I have nothing to give thee in return — only this: that I can tell thee where the Messiah must be sought. For our prophets have said that he should be born not in Jerusalem, but in Bethlehem of Judah. May the Lord bring thee in safety to that place, because thou hast had pity upon the sick."

It was already long past midnight. Artaban rode in haste, and Vasda, restored by the brief rest, ran eagerly through the silent plain and swam the channels of the river. She put forth the remnant of her strength and fled over the ground like a gazelle.

But the first beam of the rising sun sent a long shadow before her as she entered upon the final stadium of the journey, and the eyes of Artaban, anxiously scanning, could discern no trace of his friends.

The many-colored terraces of black and orange and red and yellow and green and blue and white, shattered by the convulsions of nature, and crumbling under the repeated blows of human violence, still glittered like a ruined rainbow in the morning light.

Artaban rode swiftly around the hill. He dismounted and climbed to the highest terrace, looking out toward the west. But there was no sign of the caravan of the Wise Men, far or near.

At the edge of the terrace he saw a little cairn of broken bricks, and under them a piece of papyrus. He caught it up and read: "We have waited past the midnight, and can delay no longer. We go to find the King. Follow us across the desert."

Artaban sat down upon the ground and covered his head in despair.

"How can I cross the desert," said he, "with no food and a spent horse? I must return to Babylon, sell my sapphire, and buy a train of camels, and provision for the journey. I may never overtake my friends. Only God the merciful knows whether I shall not lose the sight of the King because I tarried to show mercy."

III.

Through heat and cold, the Magian moved steadily onward until he arrived at Bethlehem. And it was the third day after the three Wise Men had come to that place and had found Mary and Joseph, with the young child, Jesus, and had laid their gifts of gold and frankincense and myrrh at his feet.

Then the Other Wise Man drew near, weary, but full of hope, bearing his ruby and his pearl to offer to the King. "For now at last," he said, "I shall surely find him, though I be alone, and later than my brethren. This is the place of which the Hebrew exile told me that the prophets had spoken, and here I shall behold the rising of the great light. But I must inquire about the visit of my brethren, and to what house the star directed them, and to whom they presented their tribute."

The streets of the village seemed to be deserted, and Artaban wondered whether the men had all gone up to the hill pastures to bring down their sheep. From the open door of a cottage he heard the sound of a woman's voice singing softly. He entered and found a young mother hushing her baby to rest. She told him of the strangers from the far East who had appeared in the village three days ago, and how they said that a star had guided them to the place where Joseph of Nazareth was lodging with his wife and her newborn child, and how they had paid reverence to the child and given him many rich gifts.

"But the travelers disappeared again," she continued, "as suddenly as they had come. We were afraid at the strangeness of their visit. We could not understand it. The man of Nazareth took the child and his mother, and fled away that same night secretly, and it was whispered that they were going to Egypt. Ever since, there has been a spell upon the village; something evil hangs over it. They say that the Roman soldiers are coming from Jerusalem to force a new tax from us, and the men have driven the flocks and herds far back among the hills, and hidden themselves to escape it."

Artaban listened to her gentle, timid speech, and the child in her arms looked up in his face and smiled, stretching out its rosy hands to grasp at the winged circle of gold on his breast. His heart warmed to the touch. It seemed like a greeting of love and trust to one who had journeyed long in loneliness and perplexity, fighting with his own doubts and fears, and following a light that was veiled in clouds.

"Why might not this child have been the promised Prince?" he asked within himself, as he touched its soft cheek. "Kings have been born ere now in lowlier houses than this, and the favorite of the stars may rise even from a cottage. But it has not seemed good to the God of wisdom to reward my search so soon and so easily. The one whom I seek has gone before me; and now I must follow the King to Egypt."

The young mother laid the baby in its cradle, and rose to minister to the wants of the strange guest that fate had brought into her house. She set food before him, the plain fare of peasants, but willingly offered, and therefore full of refreshment for the soul as well as for the body. Artaban accepted it gratefully; and, as he ate, the child fell into a happy slumber, and murmured sweetly in its dreams, and a great peace filled the room.

But suddenly there came the noise of a wild confusion in the streets of the village, a shrieking and wailing of women's voices, a clangor of brazen trumpets and a clashing of swords, and a desperate cry: "The soldiers! The soldiers of Herod!" They are killing our children."

The young mother's face grew white with terror. She clasped her child to her bosom, and crouched motionless in the darkest corner of the room, covering him with the folds of her robe, lest he should wake and cry.

But Artaban went quickly and stood in the doorway of the house. His broad shoulders filled the portal from side to side, and the peak of his white cap all but touched the lintel.

The soldiers came hurrying down the street with bloody hands and dripping swords. At the sight of the stranger in his imposing dress they hesitated with surprise. The captain of the band approached the threshold to thrust him aside. But Artaban did not stir. His face was as calm as though he were watching the stars, and in his eyes there burned that steady radiance before which even the half-tamed hunting leopard shrinks, and the bloodhound pauses in his leap. He held the soldier silently for an instant, and then said in a low voice:

"I am all alone in this place, and I am waiting to give this jewel to the prudent captain who will leave me in peace."

He showed the ruby, glistening in the hollow of his hand like a great drop of blood.

The captain was amazed at the splendor of the gem. The pupils of his eyes expanded with desire, and the hard lines of greed wrinkled around his lips. He stretched out his hand and took the ruby.

"March on!" he cried to his men; "there is no child here. The house is empty."

The clamor and the clang of arms passed down the street. Artaban re-entered the cottage. He turned his face to the east and prayed:

"God of truth, forgive my sin! I have said the thing that is not, to save the life of a child. And two of my gifts are gone. I have spent for man that which was meant for God. Shall I ever be worthy to see the face of the King?"

But the voice of the woman, weeping for joy in the shadow behind him, said very gently:

"Because thou hast saved the life of my little one, may the Lord bless thee and keep thee; the Lord make His face to shine upon thee and be gracious unto thee; the Lord lift up His countenance upon thee and give thee peace."

IV.

The years of Artaban were flowing very swiftly as he searched for the King. He was seen among the throngs of men in populous Egypt, seeking everywhere for traces of the household that had come down from Bethlehem, and finding them under the spreading sycamore trees of Heliopolis, and beneath the walls of the Roman fortress of New Babylon beside the Nile — traces so faint and dim that they vanished before him continually, as footprints on the wet river sand glisten for a moment with moisture and then disappear. He searched through Egypt. In Alexandria he took counsel with a Hebrew rabbi. The venerable man, bending over the rolls of parchment on which the prophecies of Israel were written, read aloud the pathetic words which foretold the sufferings of the promised Messiah — the despised and rejected of men, the man of sorrows and acquainted with grief.

"And remember, my son," said he, fixing his eyes upon the face of Artaban, "the King whom thou seekest is not to be found in a palace, nor among the rich and powerful. But the light for which the world is waiting is a new light, the glory that shall rise out of patient and triumphant suffering. And the kingdom which is to be established forever is a new kingdom, the royalty of unconquerable love.

"I do not know how this shall come to pass, nor how the turbulent kings and peoples of earth shall be brought to acknowledge the Messiah and pay homage to him. But this I know. Those who seek him will do well to look among the poor and the lowly, the sorrowful and the oppressed."

So the Other Wise Man traveled from place to place, searching among the people of the Dispersion, with whom the little family from Bethlehem might, perhaps, have found a refuge. He passed through countries where famine lay heavy upon the land, and the poor were crying for bread. He made his dwelling in plague-stricken cities where the sick were languishing in the bitter companionship of helpless misery. He visited the oppressed and the afflicted in the gloom of subterranean prisons, and the crowded wretchedness of slave markets, and the weary toil of galley ships. In all this populous and intricate world of anguish, though he found none to worship, he found many to help. He fed the hungry, and clothed the naked, and healed the sick, and comforted the captive; and his years passed more swiftly than the weaver's shuttle that flashes back and forth through the loom while the web grows and the pattern is completed.

It seemed almost as if he had forgotten his quest.

V.

Three-and-thirty years of the life of Artaban had passed away, and he was still a pilgrim and a seeker after light. His hair, once darker than the cliffs of Zagros, was now white as the wintry snow that covered them. His eyes, that once flashed like flames of fire, were dull as embers smoldering among the ashes.

Worn and weary and ready to die, but still looking for the King, he had come for the last time to Jerusalem. He had often visited the Holy City before, and had searched all its lanes and crowded hovels and black prisons without finding any trace of the family of Nazarenes who had fled from Bethlehem long ago. But now it seemed as if he must make one more effort, and something whispered in his heart that, at last, he might succeed.

It was the season of the Passover. The city was thronged with strangers. The children of Israel, scattered in far lands, had returned to the Temple for the great feast, and there had been a confusion of tongues in the narrow streets for many days.

But on this day a singular agitation was visible in the multitude. The sky was veiled with a portentous gloom. Currents of excitement seemed to flash through the crowd. A secret tide was sweeping them all one way. The clatter of sandals and the soft, thick sound of thousands of bare feet shuffling over the stones, flowed unceasingly along the street that leads to the Damascus gate.

Artaban joined a group of people from his own country, Parthian Jews who had come up to keep the Passover, and inquired of them the cause of the tumult, and where they were going.

"We are going," they answered, "to the place called Golgotha, outside the city walls, where there is to be an execution. Have you not heard what has happened? Two famous robbers are to be crucified, and with them another, called Jesus of Nazareth, a man who has done many wonderful works among the people, so that they love him greatly. But the priests and elders have said that he must die, because he gave himself out to be the Son of God. And Pilate has sent him to the cross because he said that he was the 'King of the Jews.'"

How strangely these familiar words fell upon the tired heart of Artaban! They had led him for a lifetime over land and sea. And now they came to him mysteriously, like a message of despair. The King had arisen, but he had been denied and cast out. He was about to perish. Perhaps he was already dying. Could it be the same who had been born in Bethlehem thirty-three years ago, at whose birth the star had appeared in heaven, and of whose coming the prophets had spoken?

Artaban's heart beat unsteadily with that troubled, doubtful apprehension which is the excitement of old age. But he said within himself: "The ways of God are stranger than the thoughts of men, and it may be that I shall find the King, at last, in the hands of his enemies, and shall come in time to offer my pearl for his ransom before he dies."

So the old man followed the multitude with slow and painful steps toward the Damascus gate of the city. Just beyond the entrance of the guardhouse a troop of Macedonian soldiers came down the street, dragging a young girl with torn dress and disheveled hair. As the Magian paused to look at her with compassion, she broke suddenly from the hands of her tormentors, and threw herself at his feet, clasping him around the knees. She had seen his white cap and winged circle on his breast.

"Have pity on me," she cried, "and save me, for the sake of the God of Purity! My father was a merchant of Parthia, but he is dead, and I am seized for his debts to be sold as a slave. Save me from worse than death!"

Artaban trembled.

It was the old conflict in his soul, which had come to him in the palm grove of Babylon and in the cottage at Bethlehem — the conflict between the expectation of faith and the impulse of love. Twice the gift which he had consecrated to the worship of religion had been drawn to the service of humanity. This was the third trial, the ultimate probation, the final and irrevocable choice.

Was it his great opportunity, or his last temptation? He could not tell. One thing only was clear in the darkness of his mind — it was inevitable. And does not the inevitable come from God?

One thing only was sure to his divided heart — to rescue this helpless girl would be a true deed of love. And is not love the light of the soul?

He took the pearl from his bosom. Never had it seemed so luminous, so radiant, so full of tender, living luster. He laid it in the hand of the slave.

"This is thy ransom, daughter! It is the last of my treasures which I kept for the King."

While he spoke, the darkness of the sky deepened, and shuddering tremors ran through the earth heaving convulsively like the breast of one who struggles with mighty grief.

The walls of the houses rocked to and fro. Stones were loosened and crashed into the street. Dust clouds filled the air. The soldiers fled in terror, reeling like drunken men. But Artaban and the girl whom he had ransomed crouched helpless beneath the wall of the Praetorium.

What had he to fear? What had he to hope? He had given away the last remnant of his tribute for the King. He had parted with the last hope of finding him. The quest was over, and it had failed. But even in that thought, accepted and embraced, there was peace. It was not resignation. It was not submission. It was something more profound and searching. He knew that all was well, because he had done the best that he could from day to day. He had been true to the light that had been given to him. He had looked for more. And if he had not found it, if a failure was all that came out of his life, doubtless that was the best that was possible. He had not seen the revelation of "life everlasting, incorruptible and immortal." But he knew that even if he could live his earthly life over again, it could not be otherwise than it had been.

One more lingering pulsation of the earthquake quivered through the ground. A heavy tile, shaken from the roof, fell and struck the old man on the temple. He lay breathless and pale, with his gray head resting on the young girl's shoulder, and the blood trickling from the wound. As she bent over him, fearing that he was dead, there came a voice through the twilight, very small and still, like music sounding from a distance, in which the notes are clear but the words are lost. The girl turned to see if someone had spoken from the window above them, but she saw no one.

Then the old man's lips began to move, as if in answer, and she heard him say in the Parthian tongue:

"Not so, my Lord! For when saw I thee an hungered and fed thee? Or thirsty, and gave thee drink? When saw I thee a stranger, and took thee in? Or naked, and clothed thee? When saw I thee sick or in prison, and came unto thee? Three-and-thirty years have I looked for thee; but I have never seen thy face, nor ministered to thee, my King."

He ceased, and the sweet voice came again. And again the maid heard it, very faint and far away. But now it seemed as though she understood the words:

"Verily I say unto thee, Inasmuch as thou hast done it unto one of the least of these my brethren, thou hast done it unto me."

A calm radiance of wonder and joy lighted the pale face of Artaban like the first ray of dawn on a snowy mountain peak. A long breath of relief exhaled gently from his lips.

His journey was ended. His treasures were accepted. The Other Wise Man had found the King.

The Nativity Story taken from the Gospels of Luke and Matthew

The Birth of Jesus Christ

ow the birth of Jesus Christ was on this wise: When as his mother Mary was espoused to Joseph, before they came together, she was found with child of the Holy Ghost (Matthew 1:18).

The angel Gabriel was sent from God unto a city of Galilee, named Nazareth, to a virgin espoused to a man whose name was Joseph, of the house of David; and the virgin's name was Mary. And the angel came in unto her, and said, "Hail, thou that art highly favored, the Lord is with thee; blessed art thou among women."

And when she saw him, she was troubled at his saying, and cast in her mind what manner of salutation this should be. And the angel said unto her, "Fear not, Mary: for thou hast found favor with God. And behold, thou shalt conceive in thy womb, and bring forth a son, and shalt call his name JESUS. He shall be great, and shall be called the Son of the Highest: and the Lord God shall give unto him the throne of his father David: and he shall reign over the house of Jacob for ever; and of his kingdom there shall be no end."

Then said Mary unto the angel, "How shall this be, seeing I know not a man?"

And the angel answered and said unto her, "The Holy Ghost shall come upon thee, and the power of the Highest shall overshadow thee:

therefore also that holy thing which shall be born of thee shall be called the Son of God. And, behold, thy cousin Elisabeth, she hath also conceived a son in her old age: and this is the sixth month with her, who was called barren. For with God nothing shall be impossible."

And Mary said, "Behold the handmaid of the Lord; be it unto me according to thy word." And the angel departed from her.

And Mary arose in those days, and went into the hill country with haste, into a city of Judah; and entered into the house of Zacharias, and saluted Elisabeth. And it came to pass, that, when Elisabeth heard the salutation of Mary, the babe leaped in her womb; and Elisabeth was filled with the Holy Ghost: and she spake with a loud voice, and said, "Blessed art thou among women, and blessed is the fruit of thy womb. And whence is this to me, that the mother of my Lord should come to me? For, lo, as soon as the voice of thy salutation sounded in mine ears, the babe leaped in my womb for joy. And blessed is she that believed: for there shall be a performance of those things which were told her from the Lord."

And Mary said, "My soul doth magnify the Lord, and my spirit hath rejoiced in God my Saviour, for he hath regarded the low estate of his handmaiden: for, behold, from henceforth all generations shall call me blessed.

"For he that is mighty hath done to me great things; and holy is his name. And his mercy is on them that fear him from generation to generation. He hath showed strength with his arm; he hath scattered the proud in the imagination of their hearts. He hath put down the mighty from their seats, and exalted them of low degree. He hath filled the hungry with good things; and the rich he hath sent empty away. He hath holpen his servant Israel, in remembrance of his mercy; as he spake to our fathers, to Abraham, and to his seed for ever."

And Mary abode with her about three months, and returned to her own house (Luke 1:26-56).

Then Joseph her husband, being a just man, and not willing to make her a public example, was minded to put her away privily. But while he thought on these things, behold, the angel of the Lord appeared unto him in a dream, saying, "Joseph, thou son of David, fear not to take unto thee Mary thy wife; for that which is conceived in her is of the Holy Ghost. And she shall bring forth a son, and thou shalt call his name JESUS: for he shall save his people from their sins."

Now all this was done, that it might be fulfilled which was spoken of the Lord by the prophet, saying, "Behold, a virgin shall be with child, and shall bring forth a son, and they shall call his name Emmanuel, which being interpreted is, God with us."

Then Joseph being raised from sleep did as the angel of the Lord had bidden him, and took unto him his wife: and knew her not till she had brought forth her firstborn son; and he called his name JESUS (Matthew 1:19-25).

And it came to pass in those days, that there went out a decree from Caesar Augustus, that all the world should be taxed. (And this taxing was first made when Cyrenius was governor of Syria.) And all went to be taxed, every one into his own city.

And Joseph also went up from Galilee, out of the city of Nazareth, into Judea, unto the city of David, which is called Bethlehem; (because he was of the house and lineage of David:) to be taxed with Mary his espoused wife, being great with child.

And so it was, that, while they were there, the days were accomplished that she should be delivered. And she brought forth her firstborn son, and wrapped him in swaddling clothes, and laid him in a manger; because there was no room for them in the inn.

And there were in the same country shepherds abiding in the field, keeping watch over their flock by night. And, lo, the angel of the Lord came upon them, and the glory of the Lord shone round about them: and they were sore afraid. And the angel said unto them, "Fear not: for, behold, I bring you good tidings of great joy, which shall be to all people. For unto you is born this day in the city of David a Savior, which is Christ the Lord. And this shall be a sign unto you; Ye shall find the babe wrapped in swaddling clothes, lying in a manger." And suddenly there was with the angel a multitude of the heavenly host praising God, and saying, "Glory to God in the highest, and on earth peace, good will toward men."

And it came to pass, as the angels were gone away from them into heaven, the shepherds said one to another, "Let us now go even unto Bethlehem, and see this thing which is come to pass, which the Lord hath made known unto us." And they came with haste, and found Mary, and Joseph, and the baby lying in a manger." And when they had seen it, they made known abroad the saying which was told them concerning this child. And all they that heard it wondered at those things which were told them by the shepherds. But Mary kept all these things, and pondered them in her heart.

And the shepherds returned, glorifying and praising God for all the things that they had heard and seen, as it was told unto them.

And when eight days were accomplished for the circumcising of the child, his name was called JESUS, which was so named of the angel before he was conceived in the womb. And when the days of her purification according to the law of Moses were accomplished, they brought him to Jerusalem, to present him to the Lord; (as it is written in the law of the Lord, "Every male that openeth the womb shall be called holy to the Lord;") and to offer a sacrifice according to that which is said in the law of the Lord, a pair of turtledoves, or two young pigeons.

And, behold, there was a man in Jerusalem, whose name was Simeon; and the same man was just and devout, waiting for the consolation of Israel: and the Holy Ghost was upon him. And it was revealed unto him by the Holy Ghost, that he should not see death, before he had seen the Lord's Christ.

And he came by the Spirit into the temple: and when the parents brought in the child Jesus, to do for him after the custom of the law, then took he him up in his arms, and blessed God, and said, "Lord, now lettest thou thy servant depart in peace, according to thy word: for mine eyes have seen thy salvation, which thou hast prepared before the face of all people; a light to lighten the Gentiles, and the glory of thy people Israel."

And Joseph and his mother marveled at those things which were spoken of him. And Simeon blessed them, and said unto Mary his mother, "Behold, this child is set for the fall and rising again of many in Israel; and for a sign which shall be spoken against; (yea, a sword shall pierce through thy own soul also,) that the thoughts of many hearts may be revealed."

And there was one Anna, a prophetess, the daughter of Phanuel, of the tribe of Asher: she was of a great age, and had lived with an husband seven years from her virginity; and she was a widow of about fourscore and four years, which departed not from the temple, but served God with fastings and prayers night and day. And she coming in that instant gave thanks likewise unto the Lord, and spake of him to all them that looked for redemption in Jerusalem (Luke 2:1-38).

Now when Jesus was born in Bethlehem of Judaea in the days of Herod the king, behold, there came wise men from the east to Jerusalem, saying, "Where is he that is born King of the Jews? for we have seen his star in the east, and are come to worship him."

When Herod the king had heard these things, he was troubled, and all Jerusalem with him. And when he had gathered all the chief priests and scribes of the people together, he demanded of them where Christ should be born. And they said unto him, "In Bethlehem of Judaea: for thus it is written by the prophet, 'And thou Bethlehem, in the land of Judah, art not the least among the princes of Judah: for out of thee shall come a Governor, that shall rule my people Israel.' "

Then Herod, when he had privily called the wise men, inquired of them diligently what time the star appeared. And he sent them to Bethlehem, and said, "Go and search diligently for the young child; and when ye have found him, bring me word again, that I may come and worship him also."

When they had heard the king, they departed; and, lo, the star, which they saw in the east, went before them, till it came and stood over where the young child was. When they saw the star, they rejoiced with exceeding great joy. And when they were come into the house, they saw the young child with Mary his mother, and fell down, and worshiped him: and when they had opened their treasures, they presented unto him gifts; gold, and frankincense, and myrrh. And being warned of God in a dream that they should not return to Herod, they departed into their own country another way.

And when they were departed, behold, the angel of the Lord appeareth to Joseph in a dream, saying, "Arise, and take the young child and his mother, and flee into Egypt; and be thou there until I bring thee word: for Herod will seek the young child to destroy him."

When he arose, he took the young child and his mother by night, and departed into Egypt: and was there until the death of Herod: that it might be fulfilled which was spoken of the Lord by the prophet, saying, "Out of Egypt have I called my son" (Matthew 2:1-15).

And when they had performed all things according to the law of the Lord, they returned into Galilee, to their own city Nazareth. And the child grew, and waxed strong in spirit, filled with wisdom: and the grace of God was upon him (Luke 2:39-40).

HENDRIK WILLEM VAN LOON

The Palace and the Stable

It was the seven hundred and fifty-third year since the founding of Rome.

Gaius Julius Caesar Octavianus Augustus was living in the palace of the Palatine Hill, busily engaged upon the task of ruling his empire.

In a little village of distant Syria, Mary, the wife of Joseph the carpenter, was tending her little boy, born in a stable of Bethlehem.

This is a strange world.

Before long, the palace and the stable were to meet in open combat.

And the stable was to emerge victorious.

LEO TOLSTOY

The Cobbler's Guest

There once lived in the city of Marseilles an old shoemaker, loved and honored by his neighbors, who affectionately called him "Father Martin."

One Christmas Eve, as he sat alone in his little shop reading of the visit of the wise men to the infant Jesus, and of the gifts they brought, he said to himself. "If tomorrow were the first Christmas, and if Jesus were to be born in Marseilles this night, I know what I would give Him!" He rose from his stool and took from a shelf overhead two tiny shoes of softest snow white leather, with bright silver buckles. "I would give Him those, my finest work."

Replacing the shoes, he blew out the candle and retired to rest. Hardly had he closed his eyes, it seemed, when he heard a voice call his name. . . . "Martin! Martin!"

Intuitively he felt a presence. Then the voice spoke again. . . "Martin, you have wished to see Me. Tomorrow I shall pass by your window. If you see Me, and bid Me enter, I shall be your guest at your table."

Father Martin did not sleep that night for joy. And before it was yet dawn he rose and swept and tidied up his little shop. He spread fresh sand upon the floor, and wreathed green boughs of fir along the rafters. On the spotless linen-covered table he placed a loaf of white bread, a jar of honey, and a pitcher of milk, and over the fire he hung a pot of tea. Then he took up his patient vigil at the window.

Presently he saw an old street-sweeper pass by, blowing upon his thin, gnarled hands to warm them. "Poor fellow, he must be half frozen," thought Martin. Opening the door he called out to him, "Come in, my friend, and warm, and drink a cup of hot tea." And the man gratefully accepted the invitation.

An hour passed, and Martin saw a young, miserably clothed women carrying a baby. She paused wearily to rest in the shelter of his doorway. The heart of the old cobbler was touched. Quickly he flung open the door.

"Come in and warm while you rest," he said to her. "You do not look well," he remarked.

"I am going to the hospital. I hope they will take me in, and my baby boy," she explained. "My husband is at sea, and I am ill, without a soul."

"Poor child!" cried Father Martin. "You must eat something while you are getting warm. No. Then let me give a cup of milk to the little one. Ah! What a bright, pretty fellow he is! Why, you have put no shoes on him!"

"I have no shoes for him," sighed the mother sadly. "Then he shall have this lovely pair I finished yesterday." And Father Martin took down from the shelf the soft little snow-white shoes he had admired the evening before. He slipped them on the child's feet . . . they fit perfectly. And shortly the poor young mother left, two shoes in her hand and tearful with gratitude.

And Father Martin resumed his post at the window. Hour after hour went by, and although many people passed his window, and many needy souls shared his hospitality, the expected Guest did not appear.

"It was only a dream," he sighed, with a heavy heart. "I did believe; but he has not come."

Suddenly, so it seemed to his weary eyes, the room was flooded with a strange light. And to the cobbler's astonished vision there appeared before him, one by one, the poor street-sweeper, the sick mother and her child, and all the people whom he had aided during the day. And each smiled at him and said. "Have you not seen me? Did I not sit at your table?" Then they vanished.

At last, out of the silence, Father Martin heard again the gentle voice repeating the old familiar words. "Whosoever shall receive one such in My name, receiveth Me . . . for I was an hungered, and ye gave Me meat; I was athirst, and ye gave Me drink; I was a stranger, and ye took Me in . . . verily I say unto you, inasmuch as ye have done it unto one of the least of these, ye have done it unto Me."

The Thorn of Glastonbury

There is a golden Christmas legend and it relates how Joseph of Arimathea — that good man and just, who laid our Lord in his own sepulcher, was persecuted by Pontius Pilate, and how he fled from Jerusalem carrying with him the Holy Grail hidden beneath a cloth of samite, mystical and white.

For many moons he wandered, leaning on his staff cut from a white thorn bush. He passed over raging seas and dreary wastes, he wandered through trackless forests, climbed rugged mountains, and forded many floods. At last he came to Gaul where the Apostle Philip was preaching the glad tidings to the heathen. And there Joseph abode for a little space.

Now, upon a night while Joseph lay asleep in his hut, he was wakened by a radiant light. And as he gazed with wondering eyes he saw an angel standing by his couch, wrapped in a cloud of incense.

"Joseph of Arimathea," said the angel, "cross thou over into Britain and preach the glad tidings to King Arvigarus. And there, where a Christmas miracle shall come to pass, do thou build the first Christian church in that land."

And while Joseph lay perplexed and wondering in his heart what answer he should make, the angel vanished from his sight.

Then Joseph left his hut and calling the Apostle Philip, gave him the angel's message. And, when morning dawned, Philip sent him on his way, accompanied by eleven chosen followers. To the water's side they went, and embarking in a little ship, they came unto the coasts of Britain.

And they were met there by the heathen who carried them before Arvigarus their king. To him and to his people did Joseph of Arimathea preach the glad tidings; but the king's heart, though moved, was not convinced. Nevertheless he gave to Joseph and his followers Avalon, the happy isle, the isle of the blessed, and he bade them depart straightway and build there an altar to their God.

And a wonderful gift was this same Avalon, sometimes called the Island of Apples, and also known to the people of the land as Yniswitren, the Isle of Glassy Waters. Beautiful and peaceful was it. Deep it lay in the midst of a green valley, and the balmy breezes fanned its apple orchards, and scattered afar the sweet fragrance of rosy blossoms or ripened fruit. Soft grew the green grass beneath the feet. The smooth waves gently lapped the shore, and water lilies floated on the surface of the tide; while in the blue sky above sailed the fleecy clouds.

And it was on the holy Christmas Eve that Joseph and his companions reached the Isle of Avalon. With them they carried the Holy Grail hidden beneath its cloth of snow-white samite. Heavily they toiled up the steep ascent of the hill called Weary-All. And when they reached the top Joseph thrust his thorn-staff into the ground.

And, lo! a miracle! the thorn-staff put forth roots, sprouted and budded, and burst into a mass of white and fragrant flowers! And on the spot where the thorn had bloomed, there Joseph built the first Christian church in Britain. And he made it "wattled all round" of osiers gathered from the water's edge. And in the chapel they placed the Holy Grail.

And so, it is said, ever since at Glastonbury Abbey — the name by which that Avalon is known today — on Christmas Eve the white thorn buds and blooms.

The Three Purses

A Legend

WHEN Saint Nicholas was Bishop of Myra, there were among his people three beautiful maidens, daughters of a nobleman. Their father was so poor that he could not afford to give them dowries, and as in that land no maid might marry without a dowry, so these three maidens could not wed the youths who loved them.

At last the father became so very poor that he no longer had money with which to buy food or clothes for his daughters, and he was overcome by shame and sorrow. As for the daughters they wept continually, for they were both cold and hungry.

One day Saint Nicholas heard of the sad state of this noble family. So at night, when the maidens were asleep, and the father was watching, sorrowful and lonely, the good saint took a handful of gold, and, tying it in a purse, set off for the nobleman's house. Creeping to the open window he threw the purse into the chamber, so that it fell on the bed of the sleeping maidens.

The father picked up the purse, and when he opened it and saw the gold, he rejoiced greatly, and awakened his daughters. He gave most of the gold to his eldest child for a dowry, and thus she was enabled to wed the young man whom she loved.

A few days later Saint Nicholas filled another purse with gold, and, as before, went by night to the nobleman's house, and tossed the purse through the open window. Thus the second daughter was enabled to marry the young man whom she loved.

Now, the nobleman felt very grateful to the unknown one who threw purses of gold into his room and he longed to know who his benefactor was and to thank him. So the next night he watched beneath the open window. And when all was dark, lo! good Saint Nicholas came for the third time, carrying a silken purse filled with gold, and as he was about to throw it on the youngest maiden's bed, the nobleman caught him by his robe, crying —

"Oh, good Saint Nicholas! why do you hide yourself thus?"

And he kissed the saint's hands and feet, but Saint Nicholas, overcome with confusion at having his good deed discovered, begged the nobleman to tell no man what had happened. Thus the nobleman's third daughter was enabled to marry the young man whom she loved; and she and her father and her two sisters lived happily for the remainder of their lives.

FRIEDRICH RÜCKERT

The Little Tree That Longed for Other Leaves

THERE was a little tree that stood in the woods through both good and stormy weather, and it was covered from top to bottom with needles instead of leaves. The needles were sharp and prickly, so the little tree said to itself —

"All my tree comrades have beautiful green leaves, and I have only sharp needles. No one will touch me. If I could have a wish I would ask for leaves of pure gold."

When night came the little tree fell asleep, and, lo! in the morning it woke early and found itself covered with glistening, golden leaves.

"Ah, ah!" said the little tree, "how grand I am! No other tree in the woods is dressed in gold."

But at evening time there came a peddler with a great sack and a long beard. He saw the glitter of the golden leaves. He picked them all and hurried away leaving the little tree cold and bare.

"Alas! alas!" cried the little tree in sorrow; "all my golden leaves are gone! I am ashamed to stand among the other trees that have such beautiful foliage. If I only had another wish I would ask for leaves of glass."

Then the little tree fell asleep, and when it woke early, it found itself covered with bright and shining leaves of glass.

"Now," said the little tree, "I am happy. No tree in the woods glistens like me."

But there came a fierce storm-wind driving through the woods. It struck the glass, and in a moment all the shining leaves lay shattered on the ground.

"My leaves, my glass leaves!" moaned the little tree; "they lie broken in the dust, while all the other trees are still dressed in their beautiful foliage. Oh! if I had another wish I would ask for green leaves."

Then the little tree slept again, and in the morning it was covered with fresh, green foliage. And it laughed merrily, and said: "Now, I need not be ashamed anymore. I am like my comrades of the woods."

But along came a mother goat, looking for grass and herbs for herself and her young ones. She saw the crisp, new leaves; and she nibbled, and nibbled, and nibbled them all away, and she ate up both stems and tender shoots, till the little tree stood bare.

"Alas!" cried the little tree in anguish, "I want no more leaves, neither gold ones nor glass ones, nor green and red and yellow ones! If I could only have my needles once more, I would never complain again."

And sorrowfully the little tree fell asleep, but when it saw itself in the morning sunshine, it laughed and laughed and laughed. And all the other trees laughed, too, but the little tree did not care. Why did they laugh? Because in the night all its needles had come again! You may see this for yourself. Just go into the woods and look, but do not touch the little tree. Why not? Because it pricks.

CELIA THAXTER
Little Piccola

In the sunny land of France there lived many years ago a sweet little maid named Piccola.

Her father had died when she was a baby, and her mother was very poor and had to work hard all day in the fields for a few sous.

Little Piccola had no dolls and toys, and she was often hungry and cold, but she was never sad nor lonely.

What if there were no children for her to play with! What if she did not have fine clothes and beautiful toys! In summer there were always the birds in the forest, and the flowers in the fields and meadows — the birds sang so sweetly, and the flowers were so bright and pretty!

In the winter when the ground was covered with snow, Piccola helped her mother, and knit long stockings of blue wool.

The snow-birds had to be fed with crumbs, if she could find any, and then, there was Christmas Day.

But one year her mother was ill and could not earn any money. Piccola worked hard all the day long, and sold the stockings which she knit, even when her own little bare feet were blue with the cold.

As Christmas Day drew near she said to her mother, "I wonder what the good Saint Nicholas will bring me this year. I cannot hang my stocking in the fireplace, but I shall put my wooden shoe on the hearth for him. He will not forget me, I am sure."

"Do not think of it this year, my dear child," replied her mother. "We must be glad if we have bread enough to eat."

But Piccola could not believe that the good saint would forget her. On Christmas Eve she put her little wooden patten on the hearth before the fire, and went to sleep to dream of Saint Nicholas.

As the poor mother looked at the little shoe, she thought how unhappy her dear child would be to find it empty in the morning, and wished that she had something, even if it were only a tiny cake, for a Christmas gift. There was nothing in the house but a few sous, and these must be saved to buy bread.

When the morning dawned Piccola awoke and ran to her shoe.

Saint Nicholas had come in the night. He had not forgotten the little child who had thought of him with such faith.

See what he had brought her. It lay in the wooden patten, looking up at her with its two bright eyes, and chirping contentedly as she stroked its soft feathers.

A little swallow, cold and hungry, had flown into the chimney and down to the room, and had crept into the shoe for warmth.

Piccola danced for joy, and clasped the shivering swallow to her breast.

She ran to her mother's bedside. "Look, look!" she cried. "A Christmas gift, a gift from the good Saint Nicholas!" And she danced again in her little bare feet.

Then she fed and warmed the bird, and cared for it tenderly all winter long; teaching it to take crumbs from her hand and her lips, and to sit on her shoulder while she was working.

In the spring she opened the window for it to fly away, but it lived in the woods near by all summer, and came often in the early morning to sing its sweetest songs at her door.

Count Franz Pocci

The Stranger Child

A Legend

THERE once lived a laborer who earned his daily bread by cutting wood. His wife and two children, a boy and girl, helped him with his work. The boy's name was Valentine, and the girl's, Marie. They were obedient and pious and the joy and comfort of their poor parents.

One winter evening, this good family gathered about the table to eat their small loaf of bread, while the father read aloud from the Bible. Just as they sat down there came a knock on the window, and a sweet voice called:

"O let me in! I am a little child, and I have nothing to eat, and no place to sleep in. I am so cold and hungry! Please, good people, let me in!"

Valentine and Marie sprang from the table and ran to open the door, saying:

"Come in, poor child, we have but very little ourselves, not much more than thou hast, but what we have we will share with thee."

The stranger Child entered, and going to the fire began to warm his cold hands.

The children gave him a portion of their bread, and said:

"Thou must be very tired; come, lie down in our bed, and we will sleep on the bench here before the fire."

Then answered the stranger Child: "May God in Heaven reward you for your kindness."

They led the little guest to their small room, laid him in their bed, and covered him closely, thinking to themselves:

"Oh! how much we have to be thankful for! We have our nice warm room and comfortable bed, while this Child has nothing but the sky for a roof, and the earth for a couch."

When the parents went to their bed, Valentine and Marie lay down on the bench before the fire, and said one to the other: "The stranger Child is happy now, because he is so warm! Good-night!"

Then they fell asleep.

They had not slept many hours, when little Marie awoke, and touching her brother lightly, whispered:

"Valentine, Valentine, wake up! wake up! Listen to the beautiful music at the window."

Valentine rubbed his eyes and listened. He heard the most wonderful singing and the sweet notes of many harps.

"Blessed Child, Thee we greet,

With sound of harp And singing sweet.

"Sleep in peace, Child so bright,

We have watched thee All the night.

"Blest the home That holdeth Thee,

Peace, and love, Its guardians be."

The children listened to the beautiful singing, and it seemed to fill them with unspeakable happiness. Then creeping to the window they looked out.

They saw a rosy light in the east, and, before the house in the snow, stood a number of little children holding golden harps and lutes in their hands, and dressed in sparkling, silver robes.

Full of wonder at this sight, Valentine and Marie continued to gaze out at the window, when they heard a sound behind them, and turning saw the stranger Child standing near. He was clad in a golden garment, and wore a glistening, golden crown upon his soft hair. Sweetly he spoke to the children:

"I am the Christ Child, who wanders about the world seeking to bring joy and good things to loving children. Because you have lodged me this night I will leave with you my blessing."

As the Christ Child spoke He stepped from the door, and breaking off a bough from a fir tree that grew near, planted it in the ground, saying:

"This bough shall grow into a tree, and every year it shall bear Christmas fruit for you."

Having said this He vanished from their sight, together with the silver-clad, singing children — the angels.

And, as Valentine and Marie looked on in wonder, the fir bough grew, and grew, and grew, into a stately Christmas Tree laden with golden apples, silver nuts, and lovely toys. And after that, every year at Christmas time, the Tree bore the same wonderful fruit.

And you, dear boys and girls, when you gather around your richly decorated trees, think of the two poor children who shared their bread with a stranger child, and be thankful.

WILLIAM CAXTON

Saint Christopher

A GOLDEN LEGEND

HRISTOPHER was a Canaanite, and he was of a right great stature, twelve cubits in height, and had a terrible countenance. And it is said that as he served and dwelled with the King of Canaan, it came in his mind that he would seek the greatest prince that was in the world, and him would he serve and obey.

So he went forth and came to a right great king, whom fame said was the greatest of the world. And when the king saw him he received him into his service, and made him to dwell in his court.

Upon a time a minstrel sang before him a song in which he named oft the devil. And the king, who was a Christian, when he heard him name the devil, made anon the sign of the cross.

And when Christopher saw that he marveled, and asked what the sign might mean. And because the king would not say, he said: "If thou tell me not, I shall no longer dwell with thee."

And then the King told him, saying: "Alway when I hear the devil named make I this sign lest he grieve or annoy me."

Then said Christopher to him: "Fearest thou the devil? Then is the devil more mighty and greater than thou art? I am then deceived, for I had supposed that I had found the most mighty and the most greatest lord in all the world! Fare thee well, for I will now go seek the devil to be my lord and I his servant."

So Christopher departed from this king and hastened to seek the devil. And as he went by a great desert he saw a company of knights, and one of them, a knight cruel and horrible, came to him and demanded whither he went.

And Christopher answered: "I go to seek the devil for to be my master."

Then said the knight: "I am he that thou seekest."

And then Christopher was glad and bound himself to be the devil's servant, and took him for his master and lord.

Now, as they went along the way they found there a cross, erect and standing. And anon as the devil saw the cross he was afeared and fled. And when Christopher saw that he marveled and demanded why he was afeared, and why he fled away. And the devil would not tell him in no wise.

Then Christopher said to him: "If thou wilt not tell me, I shall anon depart from thee and shall serve thee no more."

Wherefore the devil was forced to tell him and said: "There was a man called Christ, which was hanged on the cross, and when I see his sign I am sore afraid and flee from it."

To whom Christopher said: "Then he is greater and more mightier than thou, since thou art afraid of his sign, and I see well that I have labored in vain, and have not founden the greatest lord of the world. I will serve thee no longer, but I will go seek Christ."

And when Christopher had long sought where he should find Christ, at last he came into a great desert, to a hermit that dwelt there. And he inquired of him where Christ was to be found.

Then answered the hermit: "The king whom thou desirest to serve, requireth that thou must often fast."

Christopher said: "Require of me some other thing and I shall do it, but fast I may not."

And the hermit said: "Thou must then wake and make many prayers."

And Christopher said: "I do not know how to pray, so this I may not do."

And the hermit said: "Seest thou yonder deep and wide river, in which many people have perished? Because thou art noble, and of high stature and strong of limb, so shalt thou live by the river and thou shalt bear over all people who pass that way. And this thing will be pleasing to our Lord Jesu Christ, whom thou desirest to serve, and I hope he shall show himself to thee."

Then said Christopher: "Certes, this service may I well do, and I promise Him to do it."

Then went Christopher to this river, and built himself there a hut. He carried a great pole in his hand, to support himself in the water, and bore over on his shoulders all manner of people to the other side. And there he abode, thus doing many days.

And on a time, as he slept in his hut, he heard the voice of a child which called him —

"Christopher, Christopher, come out and bear me over."

Then he awoke and went out, but he found no man. And when he was again in his house he heard the same voice, crying —

"Christopher, Christopher, come out and bear me over."

And he ran out and found nobody.

And the third time he was called and ran thither, and he found a Child by the brink of the river, which prayed him goodly to bear him over the water.

And then Christopher lifted up the Child on his shoulders, and took his staff, and entered into the river for to pass over. And the water of the river arose and swelled more and more; and the Child was heavy as lead, and always as Christopher went farther the water increased and grew more, and the Child more and more waxed heavy, insomuch that Christopher suffered great anguish and was afeared to be drowned.

And when he was escaped with great pain, and passed over the water, and set the Child aground, he said —

"Child, thou hast put me in great peril. Thou weighest almost as I had all the world upon me. I might bear no greater burden."

And the Child answered: "Christopher, marvel thee nothing, for thou hast not only borne all the world upon thee, but thou hast borne Him who created and made all the world, upon thy shoulders. I am Jesus Christ the King whom thou servest. And that thou mayest know that I say the truth, set thy staff in the earth by thy house, and thou shalt see to-morn that it shall bear flowers and fruit."

And anon the Child vanished from his eyes.

And then Christopher set his staff in the earth, and when he arose on the morn, he found his staff bearing flowers, leaves, and dates.

Francois Coppée

The Wooden Shoes of Little Wolff

ONCE upon a time — so long ago that the world has forgotten the date — in a city of the North of Europe — the name of which is so hard to pronounce that no one remembers it — there was a little boy, just seven years old, whose name was Wolff. He was an orphan and lived with his aunt, a hard-hearted, avaricious old woman, who never kissed him but once a year, on New Year's Day; and who sighed with regret every time she gave him a bowlful of soup.

The poor little boy was so sweet-tempered that he loved the old woman in spite of her bad treatment, but he could not look without trembling at the wart, decorated with four gray hairs, which grew on the end of her nose.

As Wolff's aunt was known to have a house of her own and a woolen stocking full of gold, she did not dare to send her nephew to the school for the poor. But she wrangled so that the schoolmaster of the rich boys' school was forced to lower his price and admit little Wolff among his pupils. The bad schoolmaster was vexed to have a boy so meanly clad and who paid so little, and he punished little Wolff severely without cause, ridiculed him, and even incited against him his comrades, who were the sons of rich citizens. They made the orphan their drudge and mocked at him so much that the little boy was as miserable as the stones in the street, and hid himself away in corners to cry — when the Christmas season came.

On the Eve of the great Day the schoolmaster was to take all his pupils to the midnight mass, and then to conduct them home again to their parents' houses.

Now as the winter was very severe, and a quantity of snow had fallen within the past few days, the boys came to the place of meeting warmly wrapped up, with fur-lined caps drawn down over their ears, padded jackets, gloves and knitted mittens, and good strong shoes with thick soles. Only little Wolff presented himself shivering in his thin everyday clothes, and wearing on his feet socks and wooden shoes.

His naughty comrades tried to annoy him in every possible way, but the orphan was so busy warming his hands by blowing on them, and was suffering so much from chilblains, that he paid no heed to the taunts of the others. Then the band of boys, marching two by two, started for the parish church.

It was comfortable inside the church, which was brilliant with lighted tapers. And the pupils, made lively by the gentle warmth, the sound of the organ, and the singing of the choir, began to chatter in low tones. They boasted of the midnight treats awaiting them at home. The son of the Mayor had seen, before leaving the house, a monstrous goose larded with truffles so that it looked like a black-spotted leopard. Another boy told of the fir tree waiting for him, on the branches of which hung oranges, sugar-plums, and punchinellos. Then they talked about what the Christ Child would bring them, or what he would leave in their shoes which they would certainly be careful to place before the fire when they went to bed. And the eyes of the little rogues, lively as a crowd of mice, sparkled with delight as they thought of the many gifts they would find on waking — the pink bags of burnt almonds, the bonbons, lead soldiers standing in rows, menageries, and magnificent jumping-jacks, dressed in purple and gold.

Little Wolff, alas! knew well that his miserly old aunt would send him to bed without any supper; but as he had been good and industrious all the year, he trusted that the Christ Child would not forget him, so he meant that night to set his wooden shoes on the hearth.

The midnight mass was ended. The worshipers hurried away, anxious to enjoy the treats awaiting them in their homes. The band of pupils, two by two, following the schoolmaster, passed out of the church.

Now, under the porch, seated on a stone bench, in the shadow of an arched niche, was a child asleep — a little child dressed in a white garment and with bare feet exposed to the cold. He was not a beggar, for his dress was clean and new, and — beside him upon the ground, tied in a cloth, were the tools of a carpenter's apprentice.

Under the light of the stars, his face, with its closed eyes, shone with an expression of divine sweetness, and his soft, curling blond hair seemed to form an aureole of light about his forehead. But his tender feet, blue with the cold on this cruel night of December, were pitiful to see! The pupils so warmly clad and shod, passed with indifference before the unknown child. Some, the sons of the greatest men in the city, cast looks of scorn on the barefooted one. But little Wolff, coming last out of the church, stopped deeply moved before the beautiful, sleeping child.

"Alas!" said the orphan to himself, "how dreadful! This poor little one goes without stockings in weather so cold! And, what is worse, he has no shoe to leave beside him while he sleeps, so that the Christ Child may place something in it to comfort him in all his misery."

And carried away by his tender heart, little Wolff drew off the wooden shoe from his right foot, placed it before the sleeping child; and as best as he was able, now hopping, now limping, and wetting his sock in the snow, he returned to his aunt.

"You good-for-nothing!" cried the old woman, full of rage as she saw that one of his shoes was gone. "What have you done with your shoe, little beggar?"

Little Wolff did not know how to lie, and, though shivering with terror as he saw the gray hairs on the end of her nose stand upright, he tried, stammering, to tell his adventure.

But the old miser burst into frightful laughter. "Ah! the sweet young master takes off his shoe for a beggar! Ah! master spoils a pair of shoes for a barefoot! This is something new, indeed! Ah! well, since things are so, I will place the shoe that is left in the fireplace, and tonight the Christ Child will put in a rod to whip you when you wake. And tomorrow you shall have nothing to eat but water and dry bread, and we shall see if the next time you will give away your shoe to the first vagabond who comes along."

And saying this the wicked woman gave him a box on each ear, and made him climb to his wretched room in the loft. There the heartbroken little one lay down in the darkness, and, drenching his pillow with tears, fell asleep.

But in the morning, when the old woman, awakened by the cold and shaken by her cough, descended to the kitchen, oh! wonder of wonders! She saw the great fireplace filled with bright toys, magnificent boxes of sugar-plums, riches of all sorts, and in front of all this treasure, the wooden shoe which her nephew had given to the vagabond, standing beside the other shoe which she herself had placed there the night before, intending to put in it a handful of switches.

And as little Wolff, who had come running at the cries of his aunt, stood in speechless delight before all the splendid Christmas gifts, there came great shouts of laughter from the street.

The old woman and the little boy went out to learn what it was all about, and saw the gossips gathered around the public fountain. What could have happened? Oh, a most amusing and extraordinary thing! The children of all the rich men of the city, whose parents wished to surprise them with the most beautiful gifts, had found nothing but switches in their shoes!

Then the old woman and little Wolff remembered with alarm all the riches that were in their own fireplace, but just then they saw the pastor of the parish church arriving with his face full of perplexity.

Above the bench near the church door, in the very spot where the night before a child, dressed in white, with bare feet exposed to the great cold, had rested his sleeping head, the pastor had seen a golden circle wrought into the old stones. Then all the people knew that the beautiful, sleeping child, beside whom had lain the carpenter's tools, was the Christ Child himself, and that he had rewarded the faith and charity of little Wolff.

Mr. Edwards Meets Santa Claus

The days were short and cold, the wind whistled sharply, but there was no snow. Cold rains were falling. Day after day the rain fell, pattering from the roof and pouring from the eaves.

Mary and Laura stayed close by the fire, sewing their nine patch-quilt blocks, or cutting paper dolls from scraps of wrapping paper, and hearing the wet sound of the rain. Every night was so cold that they expected to see snow the next morning, but in the morning they saw only sad, wet grass.

They pressed their noses against the squares of glass in the windows that Pa had made, and they were glad they could see out. But they wished they could see snow.

Laura was anxious because Christmas was near, and Santa Claus and his reindeer could not travel without snow. Mary was afraid that, even if it snowed, Santa Claus could not find them, so far away in Indian territory.

When they asked Ma about this, she said she didn't know.

"What day is it?" they asked her, anxiously. "How many more days until Christmas?" And they counted off the days on their fingers, till there was only one more day left.

Rain was still falling that morning. There was not one crack in the gray sky. They felt almost sure there would be no Christmas. Still, they kept hoping.

Just before noon the light changed. The clouds broke and drifted apart, shining white in a clear blue sky. The sun shone, birds sang, and thousands of drops of water sparkled on the grasses. But when Ma opened the door to let in the fresh, cold air, they heard the creek roaring.

They had not thought about the creek. Now they knew they would have no Christmas, because Santa Claus could not cross that roaring creek.

Pa came in, bringing a fat turkey. If it weighed less than twenty pounds, he said, he'd eat it, feathers and all. He asked Laura, "How's that for a Christmas dinner? Think you can manage one of those drumsticks?"

She said, yes, she could. But she was sober. Then Mary asked him if the creek was going down, and he said it was still rising.

Ma said it was too bad. She hated to think of Mr. Edwards eating his bachelor cooking all alone on Christmas day. Mr. Edwards had been asked to eat Christmas dinner with them, but Pa shook his head and said a man would risk his neck trying to cross that creek now.

"No," he said. "That current's too strong. We'll just have to make up our minds that Edwards won't be here tomorrow."

Of course that meant that Santa Claus could not come, either.

Laura and Mary tried not to mind too much. They watched Ma dress the wild turkey, and it was a very fat turkey. They were lucky little girls to have a good house to live in, and a warm fire to sit by, and such a turkey for their Christmas dinner. Ma said so, and it was true. Ma said it was too bad that Santa Claus couldn't come this year, but that they were such good girls that he hadn't forgotten them; he would surely come next year.

Still, they were not happy.

After supper that night they washed their hands and faces, buttoned their red-flannel nightgowns, tied their nightcap strings, and soberly said their prayers. They lay down in bed and pulled the covers up. It did not seem at all like Christmastime.

Pa and Ma sat silent by the fire. After a while Ma asked why Pa didn't play the fiddle, and he said, "I don't seem to have the heart to, Caroline."

After a longer while, Ma suddenly stood up.

"I'm going to hang up your stockings, girls," she said. "Maybe something will happen."

Laura's heart jumped. But then she thought again of the creek and she knew nothing could happen.

Ma took one of Mary's clean stockings and one of Laura's, and she hung them from the mantelshelf, on either side of the fireplace. Laura and Mary watched her over the edge of their bedcovers.

"Now go to sleep," Ma said, kissing them good night. "Morning will come quicker if you are asleep."

She sat down by the fire and Laura almost went to sleep. She woke up a little when she heard Pa say, "You've only made it worse, Caroline."

And she thought she heard Ma say, "No, Charles, There's the white sugar." But perhaps she was dreaming.

Then she heard Jack growl savagely. The doorlatch rattled and someone said, "Ingalls! Ingalls!" Pa was stirring up the fire, and when he opened the door Laura saw that it was morning. The outdoors was gray.

"Great fishhooks, Edwards! Come in, man! What's happened?" he exclaimed.

Laura saw the stocking limply dangling, and she scrooged her shut eyes into the pillow. She heard Pa piling wood on the fire, and she heard Mr. Edwards say he had carried his clothes on his head when he swam the creek. His teeth rattled and his voice shivered. He would be all right, he said, when he got warm.

"Your little ones ought to have a Christmas," Mr. Edwards replied. "No creek could stop me, after I fetched them their gifts from Independence."

Laura sat straight up in bed. "Did you see Santa Claus?" she shouted.

"I sure did," Mr. Edwards said.

"Where? When? What did he look like? What did he say? Did he really give you something for us?" Mary and Laura cried.

"Wait, wait a minute!" Mr. Edwards laughed. And Ma said she would put the presents in the stockings, as Santa Claus intended. She said they mustn't look.

Mr. Edwards came and sat on the floor by their bed, and he answered every question they asked him. They honestly tried not to look at Ma, and they didn't quite see what she was doing.

When he saw the creek rising, Mr. Edwards said, he had known that Santa Claus could not get across it. ("But you crossed it," Laura said. "Yes," said Mr. Edwards, "but Santa Claus is too old and fat. He couldn't make it, where a long, lean razorback like me could do so.") And Mr. Edwards reasoned that if Santa Claus couldn't cross the creek, likely he would come no further south than Independence. Why should he come forty miles across the prairie, only to be turned back? Of course he wouldn't do that!

So Mr. Edwards had walked to Independence. ("In the rain?" Mary asked. Mr. Edwards said he wore his rubber coat.) And there, coming down the street in Independence, he had met Santa Claus. ("In the daytime?" Laura asked. She hadn't thought that anyone could see Santa Claus in the daytime. No, Mr. Edwards said; it was night, but light shone out across the street from the saloons.)

Well, the first thing that Santa Claus said was, "Hello, Edwards!" ("Did he know you?" Mary asked, and Laura asked, "How did you know he was really Santa Claus?" Mr. Edwards said that Santa Claus knew everybody. And he had recognized Santa at once by his whiskers. Santa Claus had the longest, thickest, whitest set of whiskers west of the Mississippi.)

So Santa Claus said, "Hello, Edwards! Last time I saw you, you were sleeping on a corn shuck bed in Tennessee." And Mr. Edwards well remembered the little pair of red-yarn mittens that Santa Claus had left for him that time.

Then Santa Claus said: "I understand you're living now down along the Verdigris River. Have you ever met up, down yonder, with two little girls named Mary and Laura?"

"I surely am acquainted with them," Mr. Edwards replied.

"It rests heavy on my mind," said Santa Claus. "They are both of them sweet, pretty, good little young things, and I know they are expecting me. I surely do hate to disappoint the good little girls like them. Yet with the water up the way it is, I can't ever make it across that creek. I can figure no way whatsoever to get to their cabin this year, Edwards," Santa Claus said. "Would you do me the favor to fetch their gifts this one time?"

"I'll do that, and with pleasure," Mr. Edwards told him.

Then Santa Claus and Mr. Edwards stepped across the street to the hitching-posts where the pack mule was tied. ("Didn't he have his reindeer?" Laura asked. "You know he couldn't," Mary said. "There isn't any snow." "Exactly," said Mr. Edwards. Santa Claus travelled with a pack mule in the southwest.)

And Santa Claus uncinched the pack and looked through it, and he took out the presents for Mary and Laura.

"Oh, what are they?" Laura cried; but Mary asked, "Then what did he do?"

Then he shook hands with Mr. Edwards, and he swung up on his fine bay horse. Santa Claus rode well for a man of his weight and build. And he tucked his long white whiskers under his bandana. "So long, Edwards," he said, and he rode away on the Fort Dodge trail, leading his pack mule and whistling.

Laura and Mary were silent an instant, thinking of that.

Then Ma said, "You may look now, girls."

Something was shining bright in the top of Laura's stocking. She squealed and jumped out of bed. So did Mary, but Laura beat her to the fireplace. And the shining thing was a glittering new tin cup.

Mary had one just like it.

These new tin cups were their very own. Now they each had a cup to drink out of. Laura jumped up and down and shouted and laughed but Mary stood still and looked with shining eyes at her own tin cup.

Then they plunged their hands into the stockings again. And they pulled out two long, long sticks of candy. It was peppermint candy, striped red and white. They looked and looked at that beautiful candy, and Laura licked her stick, just one lick. But Mary was not so greedy. She didn't even take one lick at her stick.

Those stockings weren't empty yet. Mary and Laura pulled out two small packages. They unwrapped them, and each found a little heart-shaped cake. Over their delicate brown tops was sprinkled white sugar. The sparkling grains lay like tiny drifts of snow.

The cakes were too pretty to eat. Mary and Laura just looked at them. But at last Laura turned hers over, and she nibbled a tiny nibble from underneath, where it wouldn't show. And the inside of that little cake was white!

It has been made of pure white flour, and sweetened with white sugar.

Laura and Mary never would have looked in their stockings again. The cups and the cakes and the candy were almost too much. They were too happy to speak. But Ma asked if they were sure the stockings were empty.

Then they put their arms down inside them, to make sure.

And in the toe of each stocking was a shining bright, new penny!

They had never even thought of such a thing as having a penny. Think of having a whole penny for your very own. Think of having a cup and a cake and a stick of candy and a penny.

There never had been such a Christmas.

Now of course, right away, Laura and Mary should have thanked Mr. Edwards for bringing those lovely presents all the way from Independence. But they had forgotten all about Mr. Edwards. They had even forgotten Santa Claus. In a minute they would have remembered, but before they did, Ma said, gently. "Aren't you going to thank Mr. Edwards?"

"Oh, thank you, Mr. Edwards! Thank you!" they said, and they meant it with all their hearts. Pa shook Mr. Edwards' hand, too, and they shook it again. Pa and Ma and Mr. Edwards acted as if they were almost crying, Laura didn't know why. So she gazed again at her beautiful presents.

She looked up again when Ma gasped. And Mr. Edwards was taking sweet potatoes out of his pockets. He said they had helped to balance the package on his head when he swam across the creek. He thought Pa and Ma might like them, with the Christmas turkey.

There were nine sweet potatoes. Mr. Edwards had brought them all the way from town, too. It was just too much. Pa said so. "It's too much, Edwards," he said. They never could thank him enough.

Mary and Laura were much too excited to eat breakfast. They drank the milk from their shining new cups, but they could not swallow the rabbit stew and the cornmeal mush.

"Don't make them, Charles," Ma said. "It will soon be dinner time."

For Christmas dinner there was the tender, juicy, roasted turkey. There were the sweet potatoes, baked in the ashes and carefully wiped so that you could eat the good skins, too. There was loaf of salt-rising bread made from the last of the white flour.

And after all that there were stewed dried blackberries and little cakes. But these little cakes were made with brown sugar and they did not have white sugar sprinkled over their tops.

Then Pa and Ma and Mr. Edwards sat by the fire and talked about Christmas times back in Tennessee and up north in the Big Woods. But Mary and Laura looked at their beautiful cakes and played with their pennies and drank water out of their new cups. And little by little they licked and sucked their sticks of candy, till each stick was sharp-pointed on one end.

That was a happy Christmas.

JAMES WEBER LINN

The Philanthropist's Christmas

"**D**id you see this committee yesterday, Mr. Mathews?" asked the philanthropist. His secretary looked up.

"Yes, sir."

"You recommend them then?"

"Yes, sir."

"For fifty thousand?"

"For fifty thousand — yes, sir."

"Their corresponding subscriptions are guaranteed?"

"I went over the list carefully, Mr. Carter. The money is promised, and by responsible people."

"Very well," said the philanthropist. "You may notify them, Mr. Mathews, that my fifty thousand will be available as the bills come in."

"Yes, sir."

Old Mr. Carter laid down the letter he had been reading, and took up another. As he perused it his white eyebrows rose in irritation.

"Mr. Mathews!" he snapped.

"Yes, sir?"

"You are careless, sir!"

"I beg your pardon, Mr. Carter?" questioned the secretary, his face flushing.

The old gentleman tapped impatiently the letter he held in his hand.

"Do you pay no attention, Mr. Mathews, to my rule that no personal letters containing appeals for aid are to reach me? How do you account for this, may I ask?"

"I beg your pardon," said the secretary again. "You will see Mr. Carter, that that letter is dated three weeks ago. I have had the woman's case carefully investigated. She is undoubtedly of good reputation, and undoubtedly in need; and as she speaks of her father as having associated with you, I thought perhaps you would care to see her letter."

"A thousand worthless fellows associated with me," said the old man, harshly. "In a great factory, Mr. Mathews, a boy works alongside of the men he is put with; he does not pick and choose. I dare say this woman is telling the truth. What of it? You know that I regard my money as a public trust. Were my energy, my concentration, to be wasted by innumerable individual assaults, what would become of them? My fortune would slip through my fingers as unprofitably as sand. You understand, Mr. Mathews? Let me see no more individual letters. You know that Mr. Whittemore has full authority to deal with them. May I trouble you to ring? I am going out."

A man appeared very promptly in answer to the bell.

"Sniffen, my overcoat," said the philanthropist.

"It is 'ere, sir," answered Sniffen, helping the thin old man into the great fur folds.

"There is no word of the dog, I suppose, Sniffen?"

"None, sir. The police was here again yesterday, sir, but they said as 'ow —"

"The police!" The words were fierce with scorn. "Eight thousand incompetents!" He turned abruptly and went toward the door, where he halted a moment.

"Mr. Mathews, since that woman's letter did reach me, I suppose I must pay for my carelessness — or yours. Send her — what does she say — four children? — Send her a hundred dollars. But, for my sake, send it anonymously. Write her that I pay no attention to such claims." He went out, and Sniffen closed the door behind him.

"Takes losin' the little dog 'ard, don't 'e?" remarked Sniffen, sadly, to the secretary. "I'm afraid there ain't a chance of findin' 'im now. 'E ain't been stole, nor 'e ain't been found, or they'd 'ave brung him back for the reward. 'E's been knocked on the 'ead, like as not. 'E wasn't much of a dog to look at, you see — just a pup, I'd call 'im. An' after 'e learned that trick of slippin' 'is collar off — well, I fancy Mr. Carter's seen the last of 'im. I do, indeed."

Mr. Carter meanwhile was making his way slowly down the snowy avenue, upon his accustomed walk. The walk, however, was dull today, for Skiddles, his little terrier, was not with him to add interest and excitement. Mr. Carter had found Skiddles in the country a year and a half before. Skiddles, then a puppy, was at the time in a most undignified and undesirable position, stuck in a drain tile, and unable either to advance or to retreat. Mr. Carter had shoved him forward, after a heroic struggle, whereupon Skiddles had licked his hand. Something in the little dog's eye, or his action, had induced the rich philanthropist to bargain for him and buy him at a cost of half a dollar. Thereafter Skiddles became his daily companion, his chief distraction, and finally the apple of his eye.

Skiddles was of no known parentage, hardly of any known breed, but he suited Mr. Carter. What, the millionaire reflected with a proud cynicism, were his own antecedents, if it came to that? But now Skiddles had disappeared.

As Sniffen said, he had learned the trick of slipping free from his collar. One morning the great front doors had been left open for two minutes while the hallway was aired. Skiddles must have slipped down the marble steps unseen, and dodged round the corner. At all events, he had vanished, and although the whole police force of the city had been roused to secure his return, it was aroused in vain. And for three weeks, therefore, a small, straight, white bearded man in a fur overcoat had walked in mournful irritation alone.

He stood upon a corner uncertainly. One way led to the park, and this he usually took; but today he did not want to go to the park — it was too reminiscent of Skiddles. He looked the other way. Down there, if one went far enough, lay "slums," and Mr. Carter hated the sight of slums; they always made him miserable and discontented. With all his money and his philanthropy, was there still necessity for such misery in the world? Worse still came the intrusive question at times: Had all his money anything to do with the creation of this misery? He owned no tenements; he paid good wages in every factory; he had given sums such as few men have given in the history of philanthropy. Still — there were the slums. However, the worst slums lay some distance off, and he finally turned his back on the park and walked on.

It was the day before Christmas. You saw it in people's faces; you saw it in the holly wreaths that hung in windows; you saw it, even as you passed the splendid, forbidding houses on the avenue, in the green that here and there banked massive doors; but most of all, you saw it in the shops. Up here the shops were smallish, and chiefly of the provision variety, so there was no bewildering display of gifts; but there were Christmas trees everywhere, of all sizes. It was astonishing how many people in that neighborhood seemed to favor the old-fashioned idea of a tree.

Mr. Carter looked at them with his irritation softening. If they made him feel a trifle more lonely, they allowed him to feel also a trifle less responsible — for, after all, it was a fairly happy world.

At this moment he perceived a curious phenomenon a short distance before him — another Christmas tree but one which moved, apparently of its own volition, along the sidewalk. As Mr. Carter overtook it, he saw that it was borne, or dragged, rather by a small boy who wore a bright red flannel cap and mittens of the same peculiar material. As Mr. Carter looked down at him, he looked up at Mr. Carter, and spoke cheerfully:

"Goin' my way, mister?"

"Why," said the philanthropist, somewhat taken back, "I was!"

"Mind draggin' this a little way?" asked the boy, confidently, "my hands is cold."

"Won't you enjoy it more if you manage to take it home by yourself?"

"Oh, it ain't for me!" said the boy.

"Your employer," said the philanthropist, severely, "is certainly careless if he allows his trees to be delivered in this fashion."

"I ain't deliver' it, either" said the boy. "This is Bill's tree."

"Who is Bill?"

"He's a feller with a back that's no good."

"Is he your brother?"

"No. Take the tree a little way, will you, while I warm myself?"

The philanthropist accepted the burden — he did not know why. The boy, released, ran forward, jumped up and down, slapped his red flannel mittens on his legs, and then ran back again. After repeating these maneuvers two or three times, he returned to where the old gentleman stood holding the tree.

"Thanks," he said. "Say, mister, you look like Santa Claus yourself, standin' by the tree, with your fur cap and your coat. I bet you don't have to run to keep warm, hey?" There was high admiration in his look. Suddenly his eyes sparkled with an inspiration.

"Say, mister," he cried, "will you do something for me? Come in to Bill's — he lives only a block from here — and just let him see you. He's only a kid, and he'll think he's seen Santa Claus, sure. We can tell him you're so busy tomorrow you have to go to lots of places today. You won't have to give him anything. We're looking out for all that. Bill got hurt in the summer, and he's been in bed ever since. So we are giving him a Christmas tree and all. He gets a bunch of things — an air gun, and a train that goes around when you wind her up. They're great!"

"You boys are doing this?"

"Well, it's our club at the settlement, and of course Miss Gray thought of it, and she's givin' Bill the train. Come along, mister."

But Mr. Carter declined.

"All right," said the boy. "I guess, what with Pete and all, Bill will have Christmas enough."

"Who is Pete?"

"Bill's dog. He's had him three weeks now — the best little pup you ever saw!"

A dog which Bill had had three weeks — and in a neighbourhood not a quarter of a mile from the avenue. It was three weeks since Skiddles had disappeared. That this dog was Skiddles of course most improbable, and yet the philanthropist was ready to grasp at any clue which might lead to the lost terrier.

"How did Bill get this dog?" he demanded.

"I found him myself. Some kids had tin-canned him, and he came into our entry. He licked my hand, and then sat up on his hind legs. Somebody's taught him that, you know. I thought right away, 'Here's a dog for Bill!' And I took him over there and fed him, and they kept him in Bill's room two or three days, so he shouldn't get scared again and run off; and now he wouldn't leave Bill for anybody. Of course, he ain't much of a dog, Pete ain't," he added, "he's just a pup, but he's mighty friendly!"

"Boy," said Mr. Carter, "I guess I'll just go round and" — he was about to add, "have a look at that dog," but fearful of raising suspicion, he ended — "and see Bill."

The tenements to which the boy led him were of brick, and reasonably clean. Nearly every window showed some sign of Christmas.

The tree-bearer led the way into a dark hall, up one flight — Mr. Carter assisting with the tree — and down another dark hall, to a door, on which he knocked. A woman opened it.

"Here's the tree!" said the boy, in a loud whisper. "Is Bill's door shut?"

Mr. Carter stepped forward out of the darkness.

"I beg your pardon, madam," he said. "I met this young man in the street, and he asked me to come here and see a playmate of his who is, I understand, an invalid. But if I am intruding — "

"Come in," said the woman, heartily, throwing the door wide open. "Bill will be glad to see you, sir."

The philanthropist stepped inside.

The room was decently furnished and clean. There was a sewing machine in the corner, and in both the windows hung wreaths of holly. Between the windows was a cleared space, where evidently the tree, when decorated, was to stand.

"Are all the things here?" eagerly demanded the tree-bearer.

"They're all here, Jimmy," answered Mrs. Bailey. "The candy just came."

"Say," cried the boy, pulling off his red flannel mittens to blow on his fingers, "won't it be great? But now Bill's got to see Santa Claus. I'll just go in and tell him, an' then, when I holler, mister, you come on, and pretend you're Santa Claus." And with incredible celerity the boy opened the door at the opposite end of the room and disappeared.

"Madam," said Mr. Carter, in considerable embarrassment, "I must say one word. I am Mr. Carter, Mr. Allan Carter. You may have heard my name?"

She shook her head. "No, sir."

"I live not far from here on the avenue. Three weeks ago I lost a little dog that I valued very much. I have had all the city searched since then, in vain. Today I met the boy who has just left us. He informed me that three weeks ago he found a dog, which is at present in the possession of your son. I wonder — is it not just possible that this dog may be mine?"

Mrs. Bailey smiled. "I guess not, Mr. Carter. The dog Jimmy found hadn't come off the avenue — not from the look of him. You know there's hundreds and hundreds of dogs without homes, sir. But I will say for this one, he has a kind of a way with him."

"Hark!" said Mr. Carter.

There was a rustling and a snuffing at the door at the far end of the room, a quick scratching of feet.

Then: "Woof! woof! woof!" sharp and clear came happy impatient little barks. The philanthropist's eyes brightened. "Yes," he said, "that is the dog."

"I doubt if it can be, sir", said Mrs. Bailey, deprecatingly.

"Open the door, please," commanded the philanthropist, "and let us see." Mrs. Bailey complied. There was a quick jump, a tumbling rush, and Skiddles, the lost Skiddles, was in the philanthropist's arms. Mrs. Bailey shut the door with a troubled face.

"I see it's your dog, sir," she said, "but I hope you won't be thinking that Jimmy or I —"

"Madam," interrupted Mr. Cater, "I could not be so foolish. On the contrary, I owe you a thousand thanks."

Mrs. Bailey looked more cheerful. "Poor little Billy!" she said. "It'll come hard on him, losing Pete just at Christmas time. But the boys are so good to him, I dare say he'll forget it."

"Who are these boys?" inquired the philanthropist. "Isn't their action somewhat unusual?"

"It's Miss Gray's club at the settlement, sir," explained Mrs. Bailey. "Every Christmas they do this for somebody. It's not charity; Billy and I don't need charity, or take it. It's just friendliness. They're good boys."

"I see," said the philanthropist. He was still wondering about it, though, when the door opened again, and Jimmy thrust out a face shining with anticipation.

"All ready, mister!" he said. "Bill's waitin' for you!"

"Jimmy," began Mrs. Bailey, about to explain, "the gentleman —"

But the philanthropist held up his hand, interrupting her. "You'll let me see your son, Mrs. Bailey?" he asked, gently.

"Why, certainly, sir."

Mr. Carter put Skiddles down and walked slowly into the inner room. The bed stood with its side toward him. On it lay a small boy of seven, rigid of body, but with his arms free and his face lighted with joy.

"Hello, Santa Claus!" he piped, in a voice shrill with excitement.

"Hello, Bill!" answered the philanthropist, sedately.

The boy turned his eyes on Jimmy.

"He knows my name," he said, with glee.

"He knows everybody's name," said Jimmy. "Now you tell him what you want, Bill, and he'll bring it tomorrow."

"How would you like" said the philanthropist, reflectively, "an — an —" he hesitated, it seemed so incongruous with that stiff figure on the bed — "an air-gun?"

"I guess yes," said Bill, happily.

"And a train of cars," broke in the impatient Jimmy, "that goes like sixty when you wind her?"

"Hi!" said Bill.

The philanthropist solemnly made notes of this.

"How about," he remarked, inquiringly, "a tree?"

"Honest?" said Bill.

"I think it can be managed," said "Santa Claus." He advanced to the bedside.

"I'm glad to have seen you, Bill. You know how busy I am, but I hope — I hope to see you again."

"Not till next year, of course," warned Jimmy.

"Not till then, of course," assented "Santa Claus." "And now, good-bye."

"You forgot to ask him if he'd been a good boy," suggested Jimmy.

"I have," said Bill. "I've been fine. You ask mother."

"She gives you — she gives you both a high character," said "Santa Claus." "Good-

bye again," and so saying he withdrew. Skiddles followed him out. The philanthropist closed the door of the bedroom, and then turned to Mrs. Bailey.

She was regarding him with awestruck eyes.

"Oh, sir," she said, "I know now who you are — the Mr. Carter that gives so much away to people!"

The philanthropist nodded, deprecatingly.

"Just so, Mrs. Bailey," he said. "And there is one gift — or loan rather — which I should like to make to you. I should like to leave the little dog with you till after the holidays. I'm afraid I'll have to claim him then; but if you'll keep him till after Christmas — and let me find, perhaps, another dog for Billy — I shall be much obliged."

Again the door of the bedroom opened, and Jimmy emerged quietly.

"Bill wants the pup," he explained.

"Pete! Pete!" came the piping but happy voice from the inner room.

Skiddles hesitated. Mr. Carter made no sign.

"Pete! Pete!" shrilled the voice again.

Slowly, very slowly, Skiddles turned and went back into the bedroom.

"You see," said Mr. Carter, smiling, "he won't be too unhappy away from me, Mrs. Bailey."

On his way home the philanthropist saw even more evidence of Christmas gaiety along the streets than before. He stepped out briskly, in spite of his sixty-eight years; he even hummed a little tune.

When he reached the house on the avenue he found his secretary still at work.

"Oh, by the way, Mr. Mathews," he said, "did you send that letter to the woman, saying I never paid attention to personal appeals? No? Then write her, please, enclosing my check for two hundred dollars, and wish her a very Merry Christmas in my name, will you? And hereafter will you always let me see such letters as that one — of course after careful investigation? I fancy perhaps I may have been too rigid in the past."

"Certainly, sir," answered the bewildered secretary. He began fumbling excitedly for his notebook.

"I found the little dog," continued the philanthropist. "You will be glad to know that."

"You have found him?" cried the secretary. "Have you got him back, Mr. Carter? Where was he?"

"He was — detained — on Oak Street, I believe," said the philanthropist. "No, I have not got him back yet. I have left him with a young boy till after the holidays."

He settled himself to his papers, for philanthropists must toil even on the twenty-fourth of December, but the secretary shook his head in a daze. "I wonder what's happened?" he said to himself.

The Promise

There was once a harper who played such beautiful music and sang such beautiful songs that his fame spread throughout the whole land; and at last the king heard of him and sent messengers to bring him to the palace.

"I will neither eat nor sleep till I have seen your face and heard the sound of your harp." This was the message the king sent to the harper.

The messengers said it over and over until they knew it by heart, and when they reached the harper's house they called:

"Hail, harper! Come out and listen, for we have something to tell you that will make you glad."

But when the harper heard the king's message he was sad, for he had a wife and a child and a little brown dog; and he was sorry to leave them and they were sorry to have him go.

"Stay with us," they begged; but the harper said:

"I must go, for it would be discourtesy to disappoint the king; but as sure as holly berries are red and pine is green, I will come back by Christmas Day to eat my share of the Christmas pudding, and sing the Christmas songs by my own fireside."

And when he had promised this he hung his harp upon his back and went away with the messengers to the king's palace.

When he got there the king welcomed him with joy, and many things were done in his honor. He slept on a bed of softest down and ate from a plate of gold at the king's own table; and when he sang everybody and everything, from the king himself to the mouse in the palace pantry, stood still to listen.

No matter what he was doing, however, feasting or resting, singing or listening to praises, he never forgot the promise that he had made to his wife and his child and his little brown dog, and when the day before Christmas came, he took his harp in his hand and went to tell the king good-by.

Now the king was loath to have the harper leave him, and he said to him, "I will give you a horse as white as milk, as glossy as satin, and as fleet as a deer, if you will stay to play and sing before my throne on Christmas Day."

But the harper answered, "I cannot stay, for I have a wife and a child and a little brown dog; and I have promised them to be at home by Christmas Day to eat my share of the Christmas pudding and sing the songs by my own fireside."

Then the king said, "If you will stay to play and sing before my throne on Christmas Day, I will give you a wonderful tree that, summer or winter, is never bare; and silver and gold will fall for you whenever you shake this little tree."

But the harper said, "I must not stay, for my wife and my child and my little brown dog are waiting for me, and I have promised them to be at home by Christmas Day to eat my share of the Christmas pudding and sing the Christmas songs by my own fireside."

Then the king said, "If you will stay on Christmas Day one tune to play and one song to sing, I will give you a velvet robe to wear, and you may sit beside me here with a ring on your finger and a crown on your head."

But the harper said, "I will not stay, for my wife and my child and my little brown dog are watching for me; and I have promised them to be at home by Christmas Day to eat my share of the Christmas pudding, and sing the Christmas songs by my own fireside." And he wrapped his cloak about him, and hung his harp upon his back, and went out from the king's palace without another word.

He had not gone far when the little white snowflakes came fluttering down from the skies.

"Harper, stay," they seemed to say,

"Do not venture out today."

But the harper said, "The snow may fall, but I must go, for I have a wife and a child and a little brown dog; and I have promised them to be at home by Christmas Day to eat my share of the Christmas pudding and sing the Christmas songs by my own fireside."

Then the snow fell thick and the snow fell fast. The hills and the valleys, the hedges and the hollows were white. The paths were all hidden, and there were drifts like mountains on the king's highway. The harper stumbled and the harper fell, but he would not turn back; and as he traveled he met the wind.

"Brother Harper, turn, I pray;

Do not journey on today," sang the wind, but the harper would not heed.

"Snows may fall and winds may blow, but I must go on," he said, "for I have a wife and a child and a little brown dog; and I have promised them to be at home by Christmas Day to eat my share of the Christmas pudding and sing the songs by my own fireside."

Then the wind blew an icy blast. The snow froze on the ground and the water froze in the rivers. The harper's breath froze in the air and icicles as long as the king's sword hung from the rocks by the king's highway. The harper shivered and the harper shook, but he would not turn back; and by and by he came to the forest that lay between them and his home.

The trees of the forest were creaking and bending in the wind, and every one of them seemed to say:

"Darkness gathers, night is near;

Harper, stop! Don't venture here."

But the harper would not stop. "Snows may fall, winds may blow, and night may come, but I have promised to be at home by Christmas Day to eat my share of the Christmas pudding and sing the Christmas songs by my own fireside. I must go on."

And on he went till the last glimmer of daylight faded and there was darkness everywhere. But the harper was not afraid of the dark.

"If I cannot see I can sing," said he, and he sang in the forest joyously:

"Sing glory, glory, glory!

And bless God's holy name;

For 'twas on Christmas morning

The little Jesus came.

"He wore no robes. No crown of gold

Was on his head that morn;

But herald angels sang for joy

To tell a king was born."

The snow ceased its falling, the wind ceased its blowing, the trees of the forest bowed down to listen, and lo! dear children, as he sang the darkness turned to wondrous light, and close at hand the harper saw the open doorway of his own home.

The wife and the child and the little brown dog were watching and waiting, and they welcomed the harper with great joy. The holly berries were red in the Christmas wreaths; their tree was a young green pine; the Christmas pudding was full of plums; and the harper was happier than a king as he sat by his own fireside to sing:

"O glory, glory, glory!

We bless God's holy name;

For 'twas to bring His wondrous love

That little Jesus came.

"And in His praise our songs we sing,
And in his name we pray;
God bless us all for Jesus' sake,
This happy Christmas Day."

WILLIS BOYD ALLEN

Mrs. Brownlow's Christmas Party

It was fine Christmas weather. Several light snowstorms in the early part of December had left the earth fair and white, and the sparkling, cold days that followed were enough to make the most crabbed and morose of mankind cheerful, as with a foretaste of the joyous season at hand. Downtown the sidewalks were crowded with mothers and sisters, buying gifts for their sons, brothers, and husbands.

Among those who were looking forward to the holidays with keen anticipations of pleasure, were Mr. and Mrs. Brownlow, of Elm Street, Boston. They had quietly talked the matter over together, and decided that, as there were three children in the family (not counting themselves, as they might well have done), it would be a delightful and not too expensive luxury to give a little Christmas party.

"You see John," said Mrs. Brownlow, "we've been asked, ourselves, to half a dozen candy-pulls and parties since we've lived here, and it seems nothin' but fair that we should do it once ourselves."

"That's so, Clarissy," replied her husband slowly; "but then — there's so many of us, and my salary's — well, it would cost considerable, little woman, wouldn't it?"

"I'll tell you what!" she exclaimed. "We needn't have a regular grown-up party, but just one for children. We can get a small tree, and a bit of a present for each of the boys and girls, with ice cream and cake, and let it go at that. The whole thing shan't cost ten dollars."

"Good!" said Mr. Brownlow heartily. "I knew you'd get some way out of it. Let's tell Bob and Sue and Polly, so they can have the fun of looking forward to it."

So it was settled and all hands entered into the plan with such a degree of earnestness that one would have thought these people were going to have some grand gift themselves, instead of giving to others, and pinching for a month afterwards, in their own comforts, as they knew they would have to do.

The first real difficulty they met was in deciding whom to invite. John was for asking only the children of their immediate neighbors; but Mrs. Brownlow said it would be kindness, as well as polite, to include those who were better off than themselves.

"I allus think, John," she explained, laying her hand on his shoulder, "that it's just's much despisin' to look down on your rich neighbors — as if they'd got was money — as on your poor ones. Let's ask 'em all: Deacon Holsum's, the Brights, and the Nortons." The Brights were Mr. Brownlow's employers.

"Anybody else?" queried her husband, with his funny twinkle. "P'raps you'd like to have me ask the governor's family!"

"Now, John, don't you be saucy," she laughed, relieved at having carried her point. "Let's put our heads together, and see who to set down. Susie will write the notes in her nice hand, and Bob can deliver them, to save postage."

"Well, you've said three," counted Mr. Brownlow on his fingers. "then there's Mrs. Sampson's little girl, and the four Williamses, and" — he enumerated one family after another, till nearly thirty names were on the list.

Once Susie broke in, "Oh Pa, don't invite that Mary Spenfield; she's awfully stuck-up and cross!"

"Good!" said her father again. "This will be just the thing for her. Let her be coffee and you be sugar, and see how much you can sweeten her that evening."

In the few days that intervened before the twenty-fifth, the whole family was busy enough, Mrs. Brownlow shopping, Susie writing the notes, and the others helping wherever they got a chance. Every evening they spread out upon the sitting-room floor such presents as had been bought during the day. These were not costly, but they were chosen lovingly, and seemed very nice indeed to Mr. Brownlow and the children, who united in praising the discriminating taste of Mrs. B.

The tree seemed at first inclined to be sulky, perhaps at having been decapitated and curtailed; for it obstinately leaned backward, kicked over the soapbox in which it was set, bumped against Mr. Brownlow, tumbled forward, and in short, behaved itself like a tree which was determined to lie on its precious back all the next day, or perish in the attempt. At length, just as they were beginning to despair of ever getting it firm and straight, it gave a little quiver of its limbs, yielded gracefully to a final push by Bob, and stood upright, as fair and comely a Christmas tree as one would wish to see. Mr. Brownlow crept out backward from under the lower branches, and regarded it with a sigh of content. Such presents as were to be disposed of in this way were not hung upon the branches; then strings of popcorn, bits of wool, and glistening paper, a few red apples, and lastly the candles. When all was finished, which was not before midnight, the family withdrew to their beds, with weary limbs and brains, but with lighthearted anticipation of tomorrow.

"Do you s'pose Mrs. Bright will come with her children, John?" asked Mrs. Brownlow, as she turned out the gas.

"Shouldn't — wonder" — sleepily from the four-poster.

"Did Mr. Bright say anything about the invitation we sent, when he paid you off?"

Silence. More silence. Good Mr. Brownlow was asleep, and Clarissa soon followed him.

Meanwhile the snow, which had been falling fast during the early part of the evening, had ceased, leaving the earth as fair to look upon as the fleece-drifted sky above it. Slowly the heavy banks of cloud rolled away, disclosing star after star, until the moon itself looked down, and sent a soft "Merry Christmas" to mankind. At last came the dawn with a glorious burst of sunlight and church-bells and glad voices, ushering in the gladdest and dearest day of all the year.

The Brownlows were early astir, full of the joyous spirit of the day. There was a clamor of Christmas greetings, and a delighted medley of shouts from the children over the few simple gifts that had been secretly laid aside for them. But the ruling thought in every heart was the party. It was to come off at five o'clock in the afternoon, when it would be just dark enough to light the candles on the tree.

In spite of all the hard work of the preceding days, there was not a moment to spare that forenoon. The house, as the head of the family facetiously remarked, was a perfect hive of B's.

As the appointed hour drew near, their nervousness increased. Nor was the excitement confined to the interior of the house. The tree was placed in the front parlor, close to the window, and by half-past four a dozen ragged children were gathered about the iron fence of the little front yard, gazing open-mouthed and open-eyed at the spectacular wonders within. At a quarter before five Mrs. Brownlow's heart beat hard every time she heard a strange footstep in their quiet street. It was a little odd that none of the guests had arrived; but then, it was fashionable to be late!

Ten minutes more passed. Still no arrivals. It was evident that each was planning not to be the first to get there, and that they would all descend on the house and assault the doorbell at once. Mrs. Brownlow repeatedly smoothed the wrinkles out of her tidy apron, and Mr. Brownlow began to perspire with responsibility.

Meanwhile the crowd outside, recognizing no rigid bonds of etiquette, rapidly increased in numbers. Mr. Brownlow, to pass the time and please the poor little homeless creatures, lighted two of the candles.

The response from the front-yard fence was immediate. A low murmur of delight ran along the line, and several dull-eyed babies were hoisted, in the arms of babies scarcely older than themselves, to behold the rare vision of candles in a tree, just illumining the further splendors glistening here and there among the branches.

The kind man's heart warmed towards them, and he lighted two more candles. The delight of the audience could now hardly be restrained, and the babies, having been temporarily lowered by the aching little arms of their respective nurses, were shot up once more to view the redoubled grandeur.

The whole family had become so much interested in these small outcasts that they had not noticed the flight of time. Now someone glanced suddenly at the clock, and exclaimed, "It's nearly half-past five!"

The Brownlows looked at one another blankly. Poor Mrs. Brownlow's smart ribbons drooped in conscious abasement, while mortification and pride struggled in their wearer's kindly face, over which, after a moment's silence, one large tear slowly rolled, and dropped off.

Mr. Brownlow gave himself a little shake and sat down, as was his wont upon critical occasions. As his absent gaze wandered about the room, so prettily decked for the guests who didn't come, it fell upon a little worn, gilt-edged volume on the table. At that sight, a new thought occurred to him. "Clarissy," he said softly, going over to his wife and putting his arm around her, "Clarissy, seein's the well-off folks haven't accepted, don't you think we'd better invite some of the others in?" And he pointed significantly toward the window.

Mrs. Brownlow, despatching another tear after the first, nodded. She was not quite equal to words yet. Being a woman, the neglect of her party cut her even more deeply than it did her husband.

Mr. Brownlow stepped to the front door. Nay more, he walked down the short flight of steps, took one little girl by the hand, and said in his pleasant, fatherly way.

"Wouldn't you like to go in and look at the tree? Come, Puss" (to the waif at his side), "we'll start first."

With these words he led the way back through the open door, and into the warm, lighted room. The children hung back a little, but seeing that no harm came to the first guest, soon flocked in, each trying to keep behind all the rest, but at the same time shouldering the babies up into view as before.

In the delightful confusion that followed, the good hosts forgot all about the miscarriage of their plans. They completely outdid themselves, in efforts to please their hastily acquired company. Bob spoke a piece, the girls sang duets. Mrs. Brownlow had held every individual baby in her motherly arms before half an hour was over. And as for Mr. Brownlow, it was simply marvelous to see him go among those children, giving them the presents, and initiating their owners into the mysterious impelling forces of monkeys with yellow legs and gymnastic tendencies; filling the boys' pockets with popcorn, blowing horns and tin whistles; now assaulting the tree (it had been lighted throughout, and — bless it — how firm it stood now!) for fresh novelties, now diving into the kitchen and returning in an unspeakably cohesive state of breathlessness and molasses candy — all the while laughing, talking, patting heads, joking, until the kindly Spirit of Christmas Present would have wept and smiled at once, for the pleasure of the sight.

"And now, my young friends," said Mr. Brownlow, raising his voice, "we'll have a little ice cream in the back room. Ladies, first, gentlemen afterward!" So saying, he gallantly stood on one side, with a sweep of his hand, to allow Mrs. Brownlow to precede him. But just as the words left his mouth there came a sharp ring at the door-bell.

"It's a carriage!" gasped Mrs. Brownlow, flying to the front window, and backing precipitately. "Susie, go to that door an' see who 'tis. Land sakes, what a mess this parlor's in!" And she gazed with a true housekeeper's dismay at the littered carpet and dripping candles.

"Deacon Holsum and Mrs. Hartwell, Pa!" announced Susie, throwing open the parlor door.

The lady thus mentioned came forward with outstretched hand. Catching a glimpse of Mrs. Brownlow's embarrassed face she exclaimed quickly —

"Isn't this splendid! Father and I were just driving past, and we saw your tree through the window, and couldn't resist dropping in upon you. You won't mind us, will you?"

"Mind — you!" repeated Mrs. Brownlow, in astonishment. "Why of course not — only you are so late — we didn't expect — "

Mrs. Hartwell looked puzzled.

"Pardon me — I don't think I quite understand — "

"The invitation was for five, you know, ma'am."

"But we received no invitation!"

Mr. Brownlow, who had greeted the deacon heartily and then listened with amazement to this conversation, now turned upon Bob, with a signally futile attempt at a withering glance.

Bob looked puzzled as the rest, for a moment. Then his face fell, and he flushed to the roots of his hair.

"I — I — must have — forgot — " he stammered.

"Forgotten what?"

"The invitations — they're in my desk now!"

Thus Bob, with utterly despairing tone and self-abasement.

"You poor dear!" Mrs. Hartwell cried, kissing her hostess, who stood speechless, not knowing whether to laugh or cry, "so that's why nobody came! But who has cluttered — who has been having such a good time here, then?"

Mr. Brownlow silently led the last two arrivals to the door of the next room, and pointed in. It was now the kind deacon's turn to be touched.

"Into the highways!" he murmured, as he looked upon the unwashed, hungry little circle about the table.

"I s'pose," said Mr. Brownlow doubtfully, "they'd like to have you sit down with 'em, just's if they were folks — if you didn't mind?"

Mind! I wish you could have seen the rich furs and overcoat come off and go down on the floor in a heap, before Polly could catch them!

When they were all seated, Mr. Brownlow looked over to the deacon, and he asked a blessing on the little ones gathered there. "Thy servants, the masters of this house, have suffered them to come unto them," he said in his prayer. "Wilt Thou take them into Thine arms, O Father of lights, and bless them!"

A momentary hush followed, and then the fun began again. Sweetly and swiftly kind words flew back and forth across the table, each one carrying its own golden threat and weaving the hearts of poor and rich into the one fine fabric of brotherhood and humanity they were meant to form.

Outside, the snow began to fall once more, each crystaled flake whispering softly as it touched the earth that Christmas night, "Peace — peace!"

A Treasury
of Classic
Poems
for Christmas

CLEMENT C. MOORE

The inspiration for the jolly St. Nicholas in "A Visit from St. Nicholas" was based on the caretaker at the author's home in New York. Moore, a theology professor, wrote the beloved poem for his children and recited it to them and his guests on December 23, 1822. A guest requested a copy, and it appeared anonymously a year later in the Troy Sentinel, Troy, New York. *Moore, a distinguished scholar, did not acknowledge his authorship of the popular poem until many years later.*

A Visit from St. Nicholas

'Twas the night before Christmas,
when all through the house
Not a creature was stirring,
not even a mouse;
The stockings were hung
by the chimney with care,
In hopes that St. Nicholas
soon would be there;

The children were nestled all snug in
their beds,
While visions of sugarplums danced in their heads;
And mamma in her kerchief, and I in my cap,
Had just settled our brains for a long winter's nap —

When out on the lawn there rose such a clatter,
I sprang from my bed to see what was the matter.
Away to the window I flew like a flash,
Tore open the shutters, and threw up the sash;

The moon, on the breast of the new-fallen snow,
Gave a luster of midday to objects below;
When what to my wondering eyes should appear
But a miniature sleigh ad eight tiny reindeer,

With a little old driver, so lively and quick,
I knew in a moment, it must be St. Nick.
More rapid than eagles his coursers they came,
And he whistled and shouted and called them by name:

"Now Dasher! now Dancer! now Prancer! now Vixen!
On, Comet! on, Cupid! on, Donner and Blitzen!
To the top of the porch! To the top of the wall!
Now, dash away, dash away, dash away, all!"

As dry leaves that before the wild hurricane fly,
When they meet with an obstacle, mount to the sky,
So up to the housetop the coursers they flew,
With the sleigh full of toys and St. Nicholas too.

And then, in a twinkling, I heard on the roof
The prancing and pawing of each little hoof.
As I drew in my head and was turning around,
Down the chimney St. Nicholas came with a bound.

He was dressed all in fur, from his head to his foot,
And his clothes were all tarnished with ashes and soot;
A bundle of toys he had flung on his back,
And he looked like a peddler just opening his pack.

His eyes: how they twinkled! his dimples: how merry!
His cheeks were like roses, his nose like a cherry;
His droll little mouth was drawn up like a bow,
And the beard on his chin was as white as the snow.

The stump of a pipe he held tight in his teeth,
And the smoke, it encircled his head like a wreath:
He had a broad face, and a little round belly,
That shook, when he laughed, like a bowl full of jelly;

He was chubby and plump, a right jolly old elf;
And I laughed, when I saw him, in spite of myself,
A wink of his eye and a twist of his head
Soon gave me to know I had nothing to dread.

He spoke not a word, but went straight to his work,
And filled all the stockings; then turned with a jerk,
And laying his finger aside of his nose,
And giving a nod, up the chimney he rose.

He sprang to his sleigh, to his team gave a whistle,
And away they all flew like the down of a thistle;
But I heard him exclaim, ere he drove out of sight,
"Happy Christmas to all, and to all a good night!"

Henry Wadsworth Longfellow

The story of the wise men has been a favorite through the centuries.
But these Kings arrive on horseback as speedy travelers from the East!

The Three Kings

Three Kings came riding
from far away,
Melchior and Gaspar and Baltasar;
Three Wise Men out of the East
were they,
And they travelled by night and
they slept by day,
For their guide was a beautiful,
wonderful star.

The star was so beautiful, large
and clear,
That all the other stars of the sky
Became a white mist in the
atmosphere;
And by this they knew that the coming was near
Of the Prince foretold in the prophecy.

Three caskets they bore on their saddle-bows,
Three caskets of gold with golden keys;
Their robes were of crimson silk, with rows
Of bells and pomegranates and furbelows,
Their turbans like blossoming almond-trees.

And so the Three Kings rode into the West,
Through the dusk of night, over hill and dell,
And sometimes they nodded with beard on breast,
And sometimes talked, as they paused to rest,
With the people they met at some wayside well.

"Of the child that is born," said Baltasar,
"Good people, I pray you, tell us the news,
For we in the East have seen his star,
And have ridden fast, and have ridden far,
To find and worship the King of the Jews."

And the people answered, "You ask in vain;
We know of no king but Herod the Great!"
They thought the Wise Men were men insane,
As they spurred their horses across the plain
Like riders in haste, and who cannot wait.

And then they came to Jerusalem,
Herod the Great, who had heard this thing,
Sent for the Wise Men and questioned them;
And said, "Go down unto Bethlehem,
And bring me tidings of this new king."

So they rode away, and the star stood still,
The only one in the gray of morn;
Yes, it stopped, — it stood still of its own free will,
Right over Bethlehem on the hill,
The city of David, where Christ was born.

And the Three Kings rode through the gate and the guard,
Through the silent street, till their horses turned
And neighed as they entered the great inn-yard;
But the windows were closed, and the doors were barred,
And only a light in the stable burned.

And cradled there in the scented hay,
In the air made sweet by the breath of kine,
The little child in the manger lay,
The Child that would be King one day
Of a kingdom not human, but divine.

His mother, Mary of Nazareth,
Sat watching beside his place of rest,
Watching the even flow of his breath,
For the joy of life and the terror of death
Were mingled together in her breast.

They laid their offerings at his feet:
The gold was their tribute to a King;
The frankincense, with its odor sweet,
Was for the Priest, the Paraclete;
The myrrh for the body's burying.

And the mother wondered and bowed her head,
And sat as still as a statue of stone;
Her heart was troubled yet comforted,
Remembering what the Angel had said
Of an endless reign and of
David's throne.

Then the Kings rode out of the
city gate,
With a clatter of hoofs in proud
array;
But they went not back to
Herod the Great,
For they knew his malice and
feared his hate,
And returned to their homes by
another way.

CHRISTINA ROSSETTI

In the Bleak Mid-Winter

In the bleak mid-winter
Frosty wind made moan,
East stood hard as iron,
Water like a stone;
Snow had fallen,
Snow on snow,
Snow on snow,
In the bleak mid-winter,
Long ago.

Our God, heav'n cannot hold him
Nor earth sustain;
Heav'n and earth shall flee away
When he comes to reign:
In the bleak mid-winter
A Stable place sufficed
The Lord God Almighty
Jesus Christ.

Enough for him, whom cherubim
Worship night and day,
A breastful of milk
And a mangerful of hay;
Enough for him, whom angels
Fall down before,
The ox and ass and camel
Which adore.

Angels and Archangels
May have gathered there,
Cherubim and Seraphim
Thronged the air;
But only his mother
In her maiden bliss
Worshipped the beloved
With a kiss.

What can I give him,
Poor as I am?
If I were a shepherd
I would bring a lamb;
If I were a wise man
I would do my part;
Yet what I can I give him —
I would give my heart.

WILLIAM BLAKE
The Lamb

Little lamb, who made thee?
Dost thou know who made thee,
Gave thee life and bade thee feed
By the stream and o'er the mead;

Gave thee clothing of delight,
Softest clothing, woolly, bright;
Gave thee such a tender voice,
Making all the vales rejoice?

Little lamb, who made thee?
Dost thou know who made thee?
Little lamb, I'll tell thee;
Little lamb, I'll tell thee.

He is called by thy name,
For He calls Himself a Lamb;
He is meek and He is mild,
He became a little child.

I a child and thou a lamb,
We are called by His name.
Little lamb, God bless thee!
Little lamb, God bless thee!

THOMAS BAILEY ALDRICH

The Oriole's Present

Just as the moon was
fading amid her misty
rings,
And every stocking was
stuffed with childhood's
precious things,
Old Kriss Kringle looked
round, and saw on an elm-
tree bough,
High-hung, an oriole's nest,
silent and empty now.

"Quite like a stocking," he laughed, "pinned up there on the tree!
Little I thought the birds expected a present from me!"
Then old Kriss Kringle who loves a joke as well as the best,
Dropped a handful of flakes in the oriole's empty nest.

Thomas Hardy

The Oxen

Christmas Eve, and twelve of
    the clock.
'Now they are all on their knees,'
An elder said as we sat in a flock
By the embers in hearthside ease.

We pictured the meed milk
      creatures where
They swelt in their strawy pen,
Nor did it occur to one of us there
To doubt they were kneeling then.

So fair a fancy few would weave
In these years! Yet, I feel,
If someone said on Christmas Eve,
'Come; see the oxen kneel

'In the lonely barton by yonder coomb
Our childhood use to know,'
I should go with him in the gloom,
Hoping it might be so.

ROBERT FROST

A Christmas Circular Letter
Christmas Trees

The city had
    withdrawn into itself
And left at last
    the country to the country;
When between whirls
    of snow not come to lie
And whirls of foliage
    not yet laid, there drove
A stranger to our yard, who
    looked the city,
Yet did in country
    fashion in that there
He sat and waited
    till he drew us out
A-buttoning coats
    to ask him who he was.

He proved to be the city come again
To look for something it had left behind
And could not do without and keep its Christmas.
He asked if I would sell my Christmas trees;
My woods — the young fir balsams like a place
Where houses all are churches and have spires.

I hadn't thought of them as Christmas trees.
I doubt if I was tempted for a moment
To sell them off their feet to go in cars

And leave the slope behind the house all bare,
Where the sun shines now no warmer than the moon.
I'd hate to have them know it if I was.

Yet more I'd hate to hold my trees except
As others hold theirs or refuse for them,
Beyond the time of profitable growth,
The trial by market everything must come to.

I dallied so much with the thought of selling.
Then whether from mistaken courtesy
And fear of seeming short of speech, or whether
From hope of hearing good of what was mine,
I said, "There aren't enough to be worthwhile."

"I could soon tell how many they would cut,
You let me look them over."

"You could look. But don't expect I'm going to let you
have them."

Pasture they spring in, some in clumps too close
That lop each other of boughs, but not a few
Quite solitary and having equal boughs
All round and round. The latter he nodded "Yes" to,
Or paused to say beneath some lovelier one,
With the buyer's moderation, "That would do."

I thought so too, but wasn't there to
say so.
We climbed the pasture on the
south, crossed over,
And came down on the north.
He said, "A thousand."
"A thousand Christmas trees! — at
what apiece?"

He felt some need of softening that to me:
"A thousand trees would come to thirty dollars."
Then I was certain I had never meant
To let him have them. Never show surprise!

But thirty dollars seemed so small beside
The extent of pasture I would strip, three cents
(For that was all they figured out apiece),
Three cents so small beside the dollar friends
I should be writing to within the hour
Would pay in cities for good trees like those,
Regular vestry-trees whole Sunday Schools
Could hang enough on to pick off enough.

A thousand Christmas trees I didn't know I had!
Worth three cents more to give away than sell
As may be shown by a simple calculation.

Too bad I couldn't lay one in a letter.
I can't help wishing I could send you one,
In wishing you herewith a Merry Christmas.

Additional copies of this book and other titles in the Honor Books
Christmas series are available from your local bookstore.

The Greatest Christmas Ever, Clothbound Gift Edition
The Greatest Christmas Ever, Paperback
The Greatest Christmas Ever, Portable
Straight From the Heart for Christmas, by Richard Exley
The Indescribable Gift, by Richard Exley
Christmas Treasures of the Heart, by Cheri Fuller
The Candymaker's Gift, by David & Helen Haidle
God's Little Christmas Book

Tulsa, Oklahoma